Thinking About Institutions

Thinking About Institutions

Milieux and Madness

R. D. Hinshelwood

> Wherever a man goes, men will pursue him
> and paw him with their dirty institutions,
> and, if they can, constrain him to belong to
> their desperate oddfellow society.
>
> *Henry Thoreau 1854*

Jessica Kingsley Publishers
London and Philadelphia

This edition published in the United Kingdom in 2001 by
Jessica Kingsley Publishers Ltd
116 Pentonville Road, London
N1 9JB, England
and
325 Chestnut Street
Philadelphia, PA 19106, USA

www.jkp.com

Library of Congress Cataloging in Publication Data
A CIP catalog record for this book is available from the Library of Congress

British Library Cataloguing in Publication Data
A CIP catalogue record for this book is available from the British Library

ISBN 1 85302 954 8

Printed and Bound in Great Britain by
Athenaeum Press, Gateshead, Tyne and Wear

Contents

Part I Boundaries and Boundary Phenomena

Part II Acting and Thinking

Part III Relational Networks

Part IV The Alienated
Commodity and Market Psychology

Foreword

In this book, Bob Hinshelwood distils a lifetime of clinical and intellectual work to discuss the major contours of the social and psychological processes that can be found in mental health and other social and business organisations in the twentieth and twenty-first centuries. Using ideas drawn from the psychoanalytic world he examines the powerful relations that develop between groups and between individuals and their social surroundings. These relations can be creative or destructive, and can result, in turn, in personal fulfilment or personal depletion.

Why would any of us opt for the negative outcomes that have in the past plagued mental hospitals or community care services? Here he argues very convincingly that rational choices only partially capture the lived reality of these complicated organisations. The complex interplay of serial projections between groups, and the disturbing impact of chaotic clients, have all too frequently resulted in a dymanic round of destructive relations that any individual may not wish, yet somehow cannot avoid, as they are drawn along a spiral of actions and reactions.

The way to deal with such negative spirals, Bob shows in this book, is to create and sustain a climate and space for critical and analytical reflection about the social relations developing within the organisation or group. Classically this has been the province of individual therapy, but since the early years of the twentieth century, and especially since the 1940s, there has developed a community, or mutually shared model for this process of reflective enquiry, often associated with the idea of the therapeutic community. Here the free flow of inter-group relations has been encouraged, precisely so that the inevitable development of projections, splitting and so forth can be held up for scrutiny. Those directly caught up in them, and in addition the community of onlookers, may learn in this way what is happening and why.

Bob himself has been deeply involved in both therapeutic community work, and individual therapy, for more than thirty years. In a way he is not alone in this experience – it comes with age! But his unique contribution to our knowledge about these processes is his long career as a thinker and writer. He stands alone in this field in terms of the range and depth of his writings, amply illustrated in the references at the end of the book. He has taken the time and trouble to think carefully about the many aspects of these processes, and to underpin much that he argues here with deeper and more difficult work published elsewhere. Typically he has written this book in a very accessible style – sensitive as always to those with whom he is communicating. Yet the argument is clearly and securely based, and will prove an enduring and helpful contribution to that spirit of reflective enquiry to which he is so deeply committed.

Nick Manning
April, 2001

Acknowledgements

I am indebted to all those people I have worked with on therapeutic community projects that I have initiated, been involved in or have been roped into. I could say it is a list too long to include here. But just as much I would worry about leaving out someone or other unwittingly who should be here. Nevertheless, there are certain people whose colleagueship has been particularly important to me in thinking about our work: Anna Christian, Sheena Grunberg, Angela Foster, Raymond Blake, Nick Manning, Harold Bourne, David Kennard, Metello Corulli, Sue Robinson, Peter Griffiths, Janet Chamberlain, Rex Haigh, Enrico Pedriali, Mike Scott. To all these companions and so many others, and not least innumerable patients, I owe my deepest thanks. With their influence, I have filled a book with reflections, most of which may be familiar to most of my colleagues; but I hope it will find interest for those who have helped me, and for my future readers.

Introduction
Thinking and Doing

The philosophical I is not the human being,
not the human body or the human soul
with the psychological properties,
but the metaphysical subject,
the boundary (not a part) of the world.

Ludwig Wittgenstein, 1921

It might be thought that the reflections of someone who has been around therapeutic communities for more than 30 years are going to be far too infested with cobwebs for relevance today. The therapeutic community after all is an organisation which continually reinvents itself everyday – that is its nature. Well so it does. But it does not do it in a vacuum. There are certain constants. One of which is just that constant impulse towards a 'shirtsleeves informality', as David Kennard once described it. The history too is constant – all therapeutic communities have come in some line of descent from those originators in the 1940s at Northfield, Belmont and the Cassel, Fulbourn, Claybury, Dingleton, Littlemore; the special schools such as Peper Harow; Grendon Prison, and so forth. But also communities interact with each other, and are a mutual influence. They inspire and give solidarity to each other. And finally there is the ambient culture in society at large – no simple thing – which has a vastly important impact on the therapeutic community, in intriguing ways. I want this book to show that a longitudinal perspective over decades can complement the immediate spontaneous impulse to reinvent. That reflective dimension may be orthogonal and cut across the day-to-day living, but can give the therapeutic community a depth, for all that.

Although most of this work came from the practice in therapeutic communities, it does lend itself to another use. The therapeutic community is a reflective institution and therefore comes from and can transpose back into the understanding of institutions (and perhaps society) in general. So, thinking about the therapeutic community task is not just relevant to its internal preoccupation and its work with those who come for help. The therapeutic community has a contribution to make back to the world again. Potentially the therapeutic community can be a research laboratory for social science. And there have been numerous studies and PhDs on the therapeutic communities which became, for a while, almost a special branch of what used to be called medical sociology.

That feedback too I want to describe here – or at least the ways in which I have personally seen the ideas feeding back into social science. After all, the ethos of the therapeutic community is that individuals come to the community with the aim of belonging and living part of their lives there, rather than simply and passively awaiting treatment by busy professionals. So the therapeutic community makes a contribution, rather than listlessly waiting on the shelf to be used in the armamentarium of psychiatrists and social workers.

Understanding things needs theories. I like theory; but I am aware that it often sets others' teeth on edge and puts me apart in a field which is essentially intuitive and practical. Nevertheless it gives me a good sense inside to have made links that fit together in some sort of structure of thoughts which of itself gives added meaning to what we do. So if that could alienate immediate colleagues who practise in the therapeutic community field, I have to write this with as much clarity as possible; and for academics and other theory lovers I have to make the intense empiricism and practical concerns and intuition accessible too. I doubt if I have managed either of these tightropes properly, but it is the best of my abilities, and represents a kind of summary statement. One day I shall be bowing out and this is my testament to the work I have collaborated in with so many other good friends and charitable competitors.

Therefore this book is not a didactic text, a 'how-to' manual. There can be no such thing for a form of work which entails spontaneity, confronting problems with personal resources, where raising questions is of more use than implementing standard answers. I am not against such an operational stance – a specific situation demands that we put into operation certain responses. In fact I would take exactly that stance.

However, the core issue to my mind is to 'take thought', and to do so whilst occupied with the day-to-day work. That, it seems to me, is the core element of the therapeutic community – and it is, in my view, a necessary element in all human institutions if they are to remain lively and responsive ones.

The idea that thought is a form of practice in its own right is both rather obvious (all professionals must think about the problems they are posed), and at the same time rather austere and strange. If thought is an effective kind of action, it can only be so if there is a communication of those thoughts between people. Action and the 'what-to-do' impulse entails the operation of thinking, finding questions and resolving questions. This book, in its method, attempts to justify that view. The *act* of reflection, which this book represents, is a form of taking action in the therapeutic community movement. The aim of the finale of the book, the Epilogue 'Living Together', which I wrote some years ago, is to prompt the reader to wonder what a creativity that is not founded on instrumental doing might look like.

It is my belief that thought and enquiry are of themselves a potent compound that creates, changes and charges with energy the culture of an institution. Within mental health we need not merely to persist with the advice – 'keep taking the pills' – but to add and substitute the new advice: keep taking thought.

In this book too we will travel into many domains inhabited by huge numbers of huge questions. These are the fields of other psychological, sociological and philosophical disciplines and practices. I and my book cannot take them on. Nevertheless we have to acknowledge profound questions about the nature of what a person is, what mental disturbance/disorder is, what makes people stick together in groups and communities, what drives societies/institutions, and so on.

I shall start with a Prologue, which came from the attempt to convey the shock, not just of finding myself working in one of those old-fashioned mental hospitals, but of being a consultant there having some responsibility for it. I recall giving that paper (the Prologue here) – 'Demoralisation in the Hospital Community' – to a packed audience at the hospital when I was graced with the presence of many senior figures in the hospital and from management committee. Looking back, it seems an almost irresponsible paper, which could do little really in a constructive way to help the severe demoralisation. But I still think it conveys a shock arising from the quality of life to which the therapeutic community movement long ago reacted.

I had encountered large mental hospitals during my psychiatric training, 1967–69, but had worked in a day hospital, and took part in running a therapeutic community for seven years, 1969–76, before taking up that senior post back in a mental hospital again, this time as a consultant psychotherapist, 1976–93. I returned to therapeutic community work as director of a specialist unit, the Cassel Hospital, much more recently, 1993–97. So, this is a journey towards acquiring usable thoughts for thinking about organisations and institutions. I have drawn on, for this volume, the substance of a number of papers that I have given and published over more than 25 years. But I am not simply repeating or republishing them. They are mined for the ideas and questions in them, which I have tried to transpose into a coherent narrative about the therapeutic community.

The progression of the argument will rest on psychoanalytic ideas, more often than on ideas from other sources. I do not refer to the use of individual psychoanalysis, which is impractical and not particularly effective for many patients, but more their application to mental health and to the free-flowing anxiety in the system of the whole institution. Freud was pessimistic about psychoanalytic treatments of psychotic patients; but we can in my view substitute an optimism about addressing the caring institution with psychoanalytic ideas and descriptions. Those ideas will not be used in a clinical way necessarily, but developed in order to understand the way people relate and collect together in institutions. I use mostly psychoanalytic ideas because of the claim, which I accept, that psychoanalysis has the resources to dig deeper beneath the surface of human phenomena than other psychologies. Of course psychoanalytic ideas have been forged only in the treatment of individual cases, and not in the observation of, or experiment with, organisations of people. This is why psychoanalytic ideas must be applied rather than clinically 'used'.

For those well acquainted with the scene in the large mental hospitals in the 1960s and 1970s in Britain, you may wish to pass over the Prologue, and to begin with Part I. For those whose careers have been more recent, and who never had direct experience of those old institutions, it is a glimpse into a world which I for one, and many, many others, reacted against. I have reprinted this old paper to try to convey that sense of shock as it was then, and which formed a motivating reason for a career-long search for alternatives – or more correctly a search for how to think about what alternatives might be.

In order to apply these ideas to the therapeutic community experience, the first step was to institute a community meeting, a dialogue involving staff and patients in a setting which could be looked at in terms of transference and countertransference. Here the working of a therapeutic community is revealed in the process of the large group of all members, staff and patients, as a dominant psychodynamic of the large group. As the main vehicle of expression of the whole community, that meeting has a real identity and focus, and was called at times, by us, the 'community personality'. The therapeutic community[1] has thus a special feature allowing investigation of an institutional system. This feature of the therapeutic community, its regular community meeting, has the function to service the social level of the organisation, to which the individuals are collectively contributing. The investigation of those community meetings invariably focuses on the boundary between two groups, the staff and the patients. This simplifies the structure to a single relation between two groups.[2] It might be regarded as a defining feature of an institution, that it consists of more than one interacting sub-group. How the individual becomes involved in the transactions between those two groups is a part of the agency of that particular individual. Why he is mobilised to centre-stage has a wider answer – to do with the collective problems of the community.

The argument in this book starts, in Part I, with this conception of the therapeutic community. The conception is that open communication between all members of the community is in itself therapeutic. This idea brings problems of communication to the fore. My early model, instead of directing attention to how to resolve communication problems directly, took the view that there are specific obstructions to communication across boundaries which need to be studied rather than simply eradicated. Communication phenomena at boundaries, particularly between sub-groups, are given priority in the theory and in the practice.

Part II proceeds from rather later reflection, not so much the form of relating in the organisation, but the *reactions* to relations in institutions. And this develops into a more theoretical argument about thinking in an institution, and its link with action and 'acting-out'. Action is the focal importance of therapeutic communities, a feature that they hold uniquely amongst the psychotherapies, and which requires a good deal of understanding since there is no good theory of action (and its deviation into 'acting-out'). I shall demonstrate that the key feature of healthy action is that it embodies reflection, and a form of communication which is not necessarily symbolic.

In Part III we deal with a particular form of action in an institution, that of one mind on another. It is possible to observe, in an almost concrete way, the impact of minds together in a collective setting, and the consequences of this for institutions, life and therapy. I discuss in fact how relations are in effect inter-psychic action. And probably the field of social psychology as well as group psychology should be seen in terms of these phenomena which can be perceived most clearly perhaps in therapeutic communities.

Finally in Part IV, this thinking develops into wider questions on society, which need to be linked with wider issues, concerning social, industrial and economic history. The origins and the continued existence of the therapeutic community are a political statement in themselves. The therapeutic community is a commitment to a way of living together, and it exists within a general social context that is in some ways deeply antipathetic to therapeutic community principles. Therapeutic communities make a statement about ethical relations in therapy (and in life in general) and can illuminate an important perspective on the way we live together in Western society now.

Living Together was the title of the book in which the Epilogue first appeared as a chapter, and it is an attempt to grasp what an alternative society might be which is based on the ethical relations a therapeutic community stands for.

As the shelf life of my earlier book on therapeutic community work (*What Happens in Groups*, 1987) comes to an end, I have taken the opportunity to build on that experience in the light of more recent work, much of it at the Cassel Hospital, 1993–97.

This book takes forward many of those ideas I explored in 1987 – boundary phenomena, dramatisations, the types of institutional containers, and the mutual interaction between the internal worlds of individuals and the external world of the community. And reference may need to be made to that earlier work in exploring the importance for institutional life of the individual psychological mechanisms of splitting, projection, introjection and identification (Klein 1946). I have written elsewhere on those mechanisms (Hinshelwood 1989a, 1993a, 1995, 1997b) and do not wish to burden readers with that thinking again. Here I will be interested in offering, in a more systematic form, an argument about the importance of these mechanisms in social problems related to caregiving. I shall also give greater emphasis to the need to think more carefully than usual about the specific practice of therapeutic communities. And finally I am interested in the place of therapeutic communities in the social and political development of society at large over the last 50 years, and the potential contribution that the understanding of therapeutic communities can have for contemporary issues in community care, and in the understanding of society in general.

Notes

1   Within a smaller organisation, such as a therapeutic community, it is possible to consider identifiable groups in the hospital, and to reach a view on aspects of their inter-communications with each other. In that instance the therapeutic community is a research setting where these dynamics of institutions may be observed, or experienced, but within the narrower dimensions of a small organisation, and thus with a greater visibility.

2   Professional role-groups too can become confused and out of touch with each other due to distortion of communications between them. Each role-group has its characteristic functions and attitudes, shared by the members of each group (e.g. Stokes 1994). They share norms of behaviour, the history or tradition of the group, and the prior training of the members. Role-groups differ from each other in these respects.

Prologue

Demoralisation in the Hospital Community

This paper was first given to staff at Napsbury Hospital in 1978, and published (Hinshelwood 1979c) in the 'samizdat' form which *Group-Analysis* then had.

Although it was written in 1978, shortly after I had joined the staff of a large mental hospital as a consultant psychotherapist, it draws on a longish experience of more than 10 years in psychiatry and of thinking and worrying about these institutions. I arrived to take up that consultant post after a therapeutic community experience of seven years, and after my training as a psychoanalyst. Both contributed enormously to my sense of being in the presence of a wonderful observational opportunity.

Although I had encountered the large mental hospital during my psychiatric training as a registrar (1967–69), I was now a consultant and had access to the corridors of power, such as they were. One of my main findings was the sense of there being no corridor of power, and a large traditional leviathan, adrift and somehow uninfluenceable, which rendered all its inmates, patient and staff alike, helpless. I was very struck by the effect on morale of the discomfort that these institutions brought out, and the extraordinary efforts that certain members made to try to work against this sense of helplessness and to achieve changes. My experience led me on the whole to support the policy of mental hospital closure. It also supported and enhanced my own concern that institutions can sink into a disastrous state and stay trapped there without much chance of anyone getting going again. This kind of psychopathology of institutions led to my long-standing observation work to try to form a basic method to understand what happens – work recently published as *Observing Organisations* (Hinshelwood and Skogstad 2000).

These impressions are very dated now, and must be read as a particular emotional record of working in a large mental hospital, and an emotional foundation that spurred a long-standing worry about psychiatry.

Demoralisation in the Hospital Community (1979)

In the old days the personnel staffing a large mental hospital actually lived within its grounds. From the medical superintendent down, the hospital was a united community of its own. Staff members would often spend a major portion of their working lives domiciled in the hospital as well as working there. The staff and patients formed a coherent social system integrated within themselves and devoted to the common values and attitudes of the hospital.

There was enormous autonomy for each hospital organised usually quite efficiently around the autocracy of the superintendent whose position resembled more the lord of the manor than the village doctor.

This way of life disappeared with the passing, in the sixties, of the post of medical superintendent. With the enormous increase in the mobility of the staff, increasing numbers of them came from overseas and from alien cultures, many found it difficult to integrate into what had been a typical English rural way of life. The sudden turn over to treatment from custodial care meant patients were always on the move in and out. And finally, the drawing of the mental hospital service into the NHS in 1947, and the further hold established by central administration in the reorganisations since, dealt blows to the old self-sufficient way of life.

What sort of a community is left now?

In this paper I should like to describe my impressions of a large mental hospital as they have struck a consultant psychotherapist who has a viewpoint that is detached slightly from the mainstream of life in these institutions. To try to understand the air of demoralisation that abounds I shall refer to the recent St Augustine's report, also to Elizabeth Bott's paper on the fraught relations that exist between hospitals and contemporary society.

Impressions of the personality of the large mental hospital

Typically mental hospitals were built 50–150 years ago. The general ambience now in such places is fairly familiar everywhere. There is an air of degradation about the buildings and the people that one sees strolling the grounds aimlessly. There are doors with peeling paint, stray cats, people in assorted garments looking like rag dolls, rusting fire-escapes, unhelpful signposts, clusters of emergency pre-fabs and portakabins, and so on.

It is easy to pick out these depressing features when one is affected by the atmosphere of the place and knowing that these large mental hospitals have regularly been hitting the headlines with scandals and brutalities over the last decade.

This paper is concerned with these problems – with the overwhelming air of decay which dominates first impressions and which drains the life out of these places. If what I say seems unfairly gloomy, it is because I am writing about gloom. I am very aware that in many places there are more hopeful signs beneath the surface but such is the atmosphere of despair that the major efforts to improve these places are not at first noticed. The energy and the long, slow painstaking work in the administrative and political areas is not immediately apparent even though many talented people are devoting their lives to pulling the mental hospitals up by their boot-straps. Some hospitals are sowing the seeds of innovation and development. Some have managed to become show-places but this often casts further despair rather than inspiration into the rest of these institutions.

Visiting these hospitals one wonders how the people who work there face this life and their jobs. I shall attempt to look beyond the appearances to try to see how these conditions come about and how people cope with being part of them.

The gothic atmosphere of decay seeps well below the surface and beyond the tangible impact of physical gloom. For example, in Hospital A, as a consultant I became a member of the Medical Staff Committee, an august-sounding body of high-status individuals. It turned out to be not quite like that, for it included a selection of not so high-status individuals, such as junior doctors, administrators, a psychologist and so on. And as happens in such status-ridden communities it was the non-consultant members who attended regularly while the senior medical staff 'looked in'. One hears about unresolved rivalries between doctors that go back years and I was reminded of Tom Main's phrase about the 'anarchical rights of the doctor in the traditional hospital society' (Main 1946). The Medical Staff Committee in those days seemed a fair enough example of what a parliament of anarchists must be like. Discussions left the indelible impression that speakers sought to establish their personal position and professional identity rather than to press, through influence and compromise, for effective workable decisions. I soon discovered that all this mattered not at all. The Medical Staff Committee no longer had power to decide anything, nor to order executive action, nor to do anything except talk and advise anyone who cared to listen. There didn't seem many who did care to.

That of course was due to the famous reorganisation of the NHS.[1] It has meant a major reapportioning of resources with a huge build-up of administration which left the clinical services in many areas of the NHS starved of finances, office accommodation, secretarial services, status and responsibilities. It sucked into these rapidly inflated administrative departments young and inexperienced career administrators who found themselves running an untried management organisation, possessing the status of the senior medical staff and the experience of student nurses. Like the reorganisation of the social services before it, the reorganisation of the NHS is taking years to smooth itself out. In the meantime there is little effective leadership, decisive authority or experience to inspire the institution anew. Again the administrators are more concerned to find their own feet, than to provide a back-up service for others. And this is felt all the way down.

I have experienced in Hospital B a works manager. He was quite independent in his buying policy, design for windows for instance, style of furnishings and his priority for rebuilding programmes. He was influenced only by ambassadorial delegations from the administration, while the medical staff conducted their clinical interview by kind permission of the pneumatic drill operators.

In the same establishment, the portering service too seemed to have declared, as with other things, its own UDI[2] from the rest of the hospital community – as with other things, no one is in a position to take effective action on it.

Such fragmentation is the order of the day: it is the personality of such hospitals. The disarticulated rag-doll spectres that stalk the grounds reflect the life-style. In one of these hospitals a non-progressing and impotent discussion had been going on for some two years about a personalised laundry service. This grand phrase sounds like a major advance in civilised living, but what it means is simply that a person who sends clothes to the laundry actually gets back the same clothes he sends.

This did not happen in that hospital. It had been defeating the organisation to provide this simple basic service for all the longer-staying patients.

Within a crumbling organisation, individuality gets squeezed out of the individuals, human beings lose their humanity. I need not go into the problem of the nursing service – there had been numerous official enquiries into the abuse of patients. Nursing standards are low, not because no one knows good ones, but because the climate within the hospital community militates against good work.

The personalities of these old places is one of decay. The people in them are struggling to find and keep their own foothold and psychological support. But as the cliff-top crumbles into rubble, everyone fights for his own and this in turn accelerates the fragmentation.

Here is the once-cohesive hospital community brought to its knees.

The St Augustine's report

When the Report of the Inskip Committee of enquiry at St Augustine's Hospital arrived two years ago, one might have thought it would put the cat amongst the pigeons, since it was an enquiry into just such another hospital community. It did have impact, it caused a stir, the cat's fur bristled but the pigeons seem to have remained quite safe.

What happened at St Augustine's? Two indignant members of the nursing staff produced in April 1974 a pamphlet they had written called 'A Critique Regarding Policy'. They circulated this internally and the administration made what seems to have been a half-hearted attempt to deal with the points raised. The authors thought it an inadequate response and produced in February 1975 a further pamphlet, 'A Critique Regarding Policy, Part II, The Evidence'. The authors' frustration had led them to produce 'an angry, bitter, extravagantly written document containing 70 detailed allegations, many are fully proved, many others are proved in part. Few remain completely unproven' (Inskip 1976, para. 1.23). The effect of this second pamphlet was for a public enquiry to be set up by the Regional Health Authority headed by a lawyer, Mr J. Hampden Inskip QC – and the Inskip Committee produced an official report.

The original Critique by Dr Brian Ankers PhD and Mr Olleste Weston was primarily concerned with incidents of nursing malpractice. However, they were at pains to avoid victimising individual members of the nursing staff and emphasised that the source of the problem was in the overall deficiency of the organisation of the place. The official enquiry agreed with this in the strongest way – 'They [Ankers and Weston] wished the authorities to concentrate on the lack of policy' (Inskip 1976, para. 1.22).

The official enquiry confirms that there were gross defects in the administrative back-up. It became a standing joke within the hospital for requisitions to be marked 'Noted and Deferred' and nothing more to be heard. Again the laundry service was abysmal.

What is being described is a situation like the hospitals I have experienced where there is a global breaking-down of all services, clinical and support. The official enquiry traces this to the lack of policy, accepting utterly the Critique that blew the gaff. The Inskip Report says in paragraph 6.1, 'There is at present no formal body between the clinical area level in the hospital and the District Management Team. The need to create some kind of body to fill this gap is recognised not only by the District Management Team, but also by all the disciplines working in the hospital.'

The recognition of this policy gap is one thing – how to fill it is another. The power to decide and execute policy is essential to a community with a task to do. In the words of a senior consultant at Hospital B – 'It is not so much a question who has their hand on the lever of power, but that there is no lever to put one's hand on.'

The Inskip Report is extremely clear on how to create a focus of power. It is the multidisciplinary team. They recognised that in the past the medical superintendent was head of the hospital, with responsibility over all other staff within it. This has changed and

> the senior doctor, senior nurses and senior administrator were each responsible in their own sphere for the staff under them. These changing attitudes and practices received formal recognition when the post of Physician Superintendent was abandoned, in many mental hospitals, and the old system was of necessity swept away when the 'Salmon organisation' was implemented for the nursing staff and the Seebohm recommendations were implemented for social workers. From that time onwards, whether there was a Physician Superintendent in post or not, he had no authority over the nursing staff or over social work staff, each of which were responsible to their organisation. The significance of this has not percolated to all the corners of the system even now, and there is no doubt that some doctors have resented this reduction in their power. (paras. 6.24–6.25)

The Report says categorically:

If there had been true multidisciplinary team work between the professions at St. Augustine's, conditions in the long stay wards would have been much better, and this long, disrupting and expensive enquiry would have been unnecessary. (p.iii)

It also warns:

Exhortation to a multidisciplinary approach is no good without ensuring that the medical profession fully participates, and this will not be achieved without giving clear guidelines as to how this should be done, even if this does mean grasping some nettles.

Who, we are left asking, will grasp the nettles?

Hospital divisions

After a series of meetings in Hospital C, involving large numbers of the nursing administration with the senior medical staff as well as a few other heads of department thrown in, a multidisciplinary meeting limped into existence.

It became immediately anomalous. It had no clear brief, except to bring together in a face-to-face setting the main holders of administrative functions in the hospital. It was a laudable enough aim – though it turned out that the majority of doctors didn't come, and the majority of nursing administrators lacked the temerity to face anybody with anything.

As a centre of power, giving backbone and thrust to the policy-making process and to the whole community of the hospital, it rather resembled warm, damp cotton-wool. One could say some nettles had not been grasped.

It was finally castigated for its lack of definition, that it had no power and that it was accountable to no one, by a report by a Hospital Advisory Service. It should be replaced by a small executive committee of three or four people from different disciplines.

While the multidisciplinary meeting slid into existence without much opposition, because it was ineffectual and therefore unthreatening, the executive committee idea produced considerable protest. The most strongly held criticism was that doctors could not accept it without having at least four members on the committee. There was a reason why it should be four.

The Inskip Report had put its finger on the important point that people had to work together in order to create a convincing sense of purpose or policy that would inspire the best efforts of the whole community. Several disciplines going in their several directions without co-ordination could only lead to the feeling of disorganisation and lack of direction. Well this may have been the root cause of the rot at St Augustine's, but there are alternative explanations. Instead, in Hospital C there was a different kind of division. The hospital was divided up into a firm system which shared out the catchment area. Now this firm system had been pushed to such considerable lengths that it was referred to as four mini-hospitals. The impression was not of a system of four parts working together but separated for reasons of efficiency – rather it seems that the idea of four mini-hospitals was an excuse for not having to work together at all.

In that case any executive committee must have a doctor from each of the four clinical firms. Relationships seemed to be such that no doctor could easily accept being represented by a doctor from another firm.

It seems that the traditional anarchical rights of hospital doctors is a nettle that was only grasped then. In Hospital C the significance of Salmon, Seebohm and NHS reorganisation had not percolated at all. It had been avoided by separating out a mini-hospital system where medical autocracy and anarchy could remain supreme and encapsulated. Until the point was grasped by the Hospital Advisory Team.

Hospital functions

I have been describing the disintegration of life in the large mental hospital. From a high-morale, rigidly organised place of a hundred years ago it has descended to a fragmented and anarchic problem-child of con-temporary society.

Why has this spiral of decay been so difficult to put right? We have discussed a number of the influences which have struck at the fabric of the hospital community, but I want now to turn to doubts about its very purpose. For more than a decade we have lived with the idea that large mental hospitals are unwanted and there has been for a while an official government policy to close them all, in time. This always brings wry smiles to the lips of those who work in them, as if such a policy is quite impossible. But I think it also goes right home to a nagging doubt about what we are really doing, in a place like this.

Elizabeth Bott has recently written a long paper on the problematic relationship between the hospital and society at large. She based her ideas on a long acquaintance with Napsbury Hospital.

Her first impressions were based on interviews with medical staff and she found that in spite of the loyalty to the hospital there was also a perplexed kind of unhappiness about the work they were doing. She writes:

> Being wise after the event, it is my view that, what was making these doctors uncomfortable was an unarticulated sense that something the hospital was doing was not straightforward. There is a sort of dishonesty in unknowingly allowing the hospital to be used to treat and house individuals who are acting as the receptacles of the madness that their relatives cannot bear to face. (Bott 1976, p.129)

The hospital is landed in a situation where it tries to help an individual on behalf of society which really just wants to be rid of him. This is a no-win situation for the hospital and its staff. Different people think of the hospital as being there for different reasons – the staff think it should treat, the patients think of it as a refuge, the relatives as a prison. Who is right? Who knows best? Society pays for the upkeep of the place and the salaries of those who work in it – should the staff please society in the form of the relatives? Yet the staff are the experts of society, they should know best. But, it is the patient's own life, it is his choice if he just wants to run and keep running from his life situation. Should he choose what is best for himself, or should someone else?

Increasingly the emphasis in hospitals has been on offering treatment or even compelling it. This has been pursued with more and more enthusiasm over the last decade or so just because treatments seem so much more effective. But it widens the rift from society which wishes to use the hospital simply as a dumping-ground. The result, Elizabeth Bott says, is that the hospital will inevitably 'have divided loyalties, to the patient and to society, and the stage will be set for a debilitating form of conflict inside the institution' (p.138).

She states the conflict more bluntly:

> If a hospital provides medical treatment for patients as individuals but refuses to provide long-term care, it seems likely that many patients may eventually end up drifting in search of some sort of resting place...if an institution frankly accepts its task as providing a home for social rejects, it will be stigmatised as a hopeless chronic institution. (Bott 1976, p.138)

The problem is, which of these functions – treatment or care and control. Whichever is chosen there is a debilitating effect, for whatever you do not only disappoints somebody, but seems to lead them on to expect something that in fact you are not offering.

This conflict between treatment on one hand and containment (i.e. care and control) on the other has illuminated the problems of Hospital C. Looking again at this mini-hospital system, a curious thing has happened. On one hand the 'treatment' function hypertrophied, the rotating door spun faster and faster till the admission rate was 60 per cent above the average for the region. On the other hand, another firm had accumulated chronic admissions till its long-stay wards became the most crowded section of the whole hospital. These two firms appear to have polarised to opposite extremes of policy exactly in line with the dilemma that Bott refers to. Treatment or containment – it was often quite a bitter point of contention between these two firms. They seem to be pushing each other out on two diametrically opposing limbs and in this way to be converting into human squabbles a dilemma which in fact we are all stuck in. I think this happened without any of the participants realising it. It is an example, if you like, of group dynamics on a community scale.

It is this essential conflict between treatment and containment, between hospital and society and really between sanity and madness which got into the crevices of that mini-hospital system I described in Hospital C and helped to prise apart the whole structure. One of the doctors that Bott interviewed at Napsbury some time ago is quoted as saying:

> The hospital is like schizophrenia itself, split up in bits, projections all over the place, parts not communicating with other parts. Things are always getting lost in this place – people, ideas, decisions. There is an overpowering sense of inertia.

This rings a bell with what I have been describing in hospitals of my acquaintance and in the St Augustine's report.

It is the most crucial issue if there is a confusion or conflict between different purposes. When that happens an apathy and demoralisation takes over, which in spite of full loyalties, affects the life and effectiveness of the institution and the satisfaction of those who work there. They are in an impossible position that is not of their making – nor are they in a position to understand exactly what position it is they are in; nor how it has arisen.

Morale and the demoralised institution

Isabel Menzies in a recent paper on 'Staff Support Systems' describes the problems in getting straight what the purpose of the institution is and she says:

> Quite simply, unless the members of the institution know what it is they are supposed to be doing, there is little hope of their doing it effectively and getting adequate satisfactions in doing so. Lack of such definition is likely to lead to personal confusion in members of the institution, to inter-personal and inter-group conflict and to other undesirable institutional phenomena. (Menzies 1979, p.197)

The purpose of an institution may be multiple, with several functions. There *may* be a conflict of priorities or the functions may get confused with each other and not properly clarified with those who are supposed to be carrying them out. In addition, the resources of the institution may be inadequate for serving all the functions and all the needs of the patients, so that stricter priorities and more restricted definitions of the functions must be thrashed out.

In all these cases, the members of staff will either not really know exactly what they are supposed to be doing, or they will know what is expected, but also know they can't fully provide it. The cost is always in terms of the job satisfaction for the staff. They feel inadequate, with an uneasy sense of failing in their job, often hard to put a finger on exactly in what way they fail. In the course of time such uncertainty eats into the confidence of the staff collectively. They may begin to lose sight of their own roles and purpose and their sense of value to the institution. Eventually they will look around for roles which they feel will enhance the sense of adequacy and value and in turn they feel encroached on by others who are also looking round. Friction and this special form of rivalry comes to the fore, the staff seem no longer to be working for the collective purpose of the institution but rather for themselves, to find their own feet in their own jobs as they feel the foundations of their own esteem slipping away from under them. The end result is the fragmented, demoralised hospital community that I started by describing.

At this point attacks are made on the institution. It is bitterly criticised for being too slack and inefficient and also for being too arbitrary and dictatorial. A hopelessness develops, a collective shrugging of the shoulders as no one feels they are listened to or supported. There is a kind of hatred of the job, as anything which goes wrong makes the person aware of his own sense of inadequacy or insignificance. In particular patients who do not, in this ethos, confirm for the nurse that he is valued will come to be hated *by* the nurse for reminding him of his own uncertainty about himself – verbal and sometimes physical attacks may result from the nurse's anguish. Administrators too are hated if they do not confirm a person's value by jumping to his demands and satisfying his requests immediately. The administrators in turn are overwhelmed by demands to satisfy, when their job, in any case, is merely to reconcile conflicting demands.

All this is a far cry from the stability of the traditional hospital of 100 years ago when everyone had his own role, within his own capabilities, and giving him his own measured sense of value.

That rigidly organised traditional kind of community gave security to many patients seeking refuge – and it also gave security to many members of staff who found value for themselves in the well defined roles and purpose. But this won't wash today. The traditional mental hospital has been found seriously wanting because of its ability to strip patients of their own personality and individuality. Goffman (1968) takes it as a paradigm of what he calls the 'total' institution. In this there is a breakdown of the boundaries ordinarily separating the basic spheres of life – sleep, play and work. All of life is carried on in the same place, under the same authority, in the company of a large batch of others in tight schedules organised from above and all for the exclusive purpose of the institution. This kind of encroachment of the institutional demand into the most private corners of the individual is rightly condemned as inhumane and also of course not very therapeutic.

How have the recent changes, Seebohm, Salmon, scrapping the Medical Superintendent and NHS reorganisation, helped? Have they contributed to a more therapeutic form of hospital community? If the examples that I have given are anything to go by, the answer must be no. The examples suggest more a breakdown of the institution, a psychological illness of the hospital itself.

And the root of this illness we have seen is the lack of policy, purpose and morale. The old style hospital and its functions, what it does for both patients and staff, have to be replaced by something or other.

Maurice Punch, a sociologist writing on a whole movement of similar organisations, talks about the anti-institution which is a response to the defects of Goffman's 'total' institution. Punch says:

> This desire to escape what is perceived as the deleterious consequences
> of a permanent social structure in formal organisations and the attempt
> to capture the absence of constraint in an association with an

anti-authoritarian ideology is what we mean by an anti-institution. (Punch 1974, p.312)

In the field of psychiatry the local brand of anti-institution is the therapeutic community. In a nutshell he says it is an attempt to institutionalise freedom. Though he has many reservations about the self-contradictory nature of that ideology nevertheless it is an ideology, and it is available as a policy to fill a gap. By contrast, in the demoralised community there is a tendency to institutionalise failure and that will not command any allegiance from anyone.

Coping with demoralisation

It is a serious dilemma for the individual member of the hospital community that he has to work for an institution that he cannot give his allegiance to. There is not felt to be anything with which to form an allegiance. There is merely a gap, an emptiness at the core of things.

In such a gap it is everyone for himself. That is not the 'freedom' of the anti-institution but the desperation of the man on the sinking ship. Everyone has a form of spurious autonomy. It is spurious because he may have a wide scope to do exactly what he wants to, yet he receives no recognition within the institution he is part of.

How does the individual cope with this? I will mention five methods:

1. One characteristic way which I have remarked on is the creation of personal empires, mini-hospitals and autonomous sub-groups within the organisation. To enhance his security, an individual gathers around him what he can. In such groups very odd things happen as we have seen. As well as destroying the integration of the hospital the purpose adopted by the group may be very bizarre, for instance the porters who see their role as primarily standing by for emergencies rather than responding to one.

2. In other areas, for instance the clinical work, there is an inappropriately aggressive pursuit of the hospital purpose – if patients are there to be treated they will damned well get their ECT and so on. Such an attitude reflects the desperate attempts by staff to feel, and to demonstrate to others, that they are performing an essential and valued service.

3. Many people find some relief in stepping back a little and using the hospital as a kind of Aunt Sally. Often with considerable humour they can convert their own frustrations into sensations and horror stories for their friends and acquaintances. This may provide good after-dinner conversation. Or incidentally someone may decide to deliver a lurid lecture on demoralisation in mental hospitals, as an excuse for his own opportunity to abreact his frustrations.

4. Other people may step back a little further, become more indignant than amused and say, 'something must be done'. They then engage in political activity of some kind. In one of the hospitals the lack of administrative or medical lead in policy-making has led, through exasperation and some intimidation, to the clinical nursing levels throwing up an active and difficult union executive who have delivered their own policy statement and detailed recommendations for an overall hospital strategy. It is backward-looking and deeply disheartening to the medical staff, but it is the only coherent group within the hospital to have stepped into the policy gap and it has gained a considerable political allegiance for its daring.

5. Finally there are the attempts to cope with the demoralisation by seeking out the root cause and putting it right. There are two clear approaches to this. Both attempt to bridge across gaps or differences. In the first approach the root cause is seen as divisions between different groups in the hospital. The St Augustine's report saw this as the separation of the different clinical disciplines. The solution is therefore to get the divisions into contact with each other and into communication with each other. The second approach sees the root cause in the conflict of functions. The solution is therefore to try to integrate the functions into a new re-definition of the purpose of the hospital. For example, I see this approach in the efforts of Napsbury Hospital to use family and community psychiatry in a radical attempt to tackle the mutual misconceptions of the parties involved in the process of hospitalisation.

Conclusion

In conclusion, I will summarise the main points. I have taken from three sources evidence of breakdowns in hospital communities. Firstly there were my own impressions of hospitals, known to me, secondly the official report of the enquiry into St Augustine's Hospital and thirdly Elizabeth Bott's social anthropological study.

A number of factors have played a part. The changes following the Seebohm and Salmon reports on the social work and the nursing professions, the abolition of the Medical Superintendent, the advent of a transient and often foreign staff instead of permanent life-long local people, the reorganisation of the NHS in 1974, the change in the function of psychiatry to a treatment endeavour, and finally the self-defeating influence of the demoralisation itself once it gets going.

The effect is to create a community with a seriously impaired effectiveness. In particular there is a serious policy gap which deprives the members of the hospital from having an inspirational sense of purpose; and also an increasing division, ultimately a fragmentation, of the fabric of the community, so that members no longer know where they stand.

Morale within the staff depends on these two supports – a convincing sense of purpose; and a sense of securely belonging to an integrated social group that devotes itself to the purpose.

Loss of morale leads to individuals taking action for their own psychological peace of mind which in the long run increases the fragmentation and erodes any clear sense of common purpose.

Notes

1   This refers to the reorganisation of 1974.

2   Unilateral declaration of independence; the initials were familiar at the time from the political independence declared by Rhodesia.

PART I

Boundaries and Boundary Phenomena

Introduction to part one

The Prologue stated a problem. These old-fashioned institutions exist, and what should we do about them? History has moved on, and something has been done. By and large, the hospitals are all closed, or radically reduced in size, and what remains of the old buildings are now small units for rehabilitation or for highly specialist functions such as forensic psychiatry.

In the first Part of this book we will move from mere description of these old institutions to consideration of the nature of boundaries; to cultures; and to personal identity – that inward correspondent of social culture.

In Chapter 1 I shall start with the need to change those old institutions in which people were incarcerated, often for decades of their lives. Many people in the 1940s and 1950s became aware that this incarceration captured the staff in the system as surely as patients. I intend to start from the view that the physical incarceration in part symbolises a psychological imprisonment which entraps all. Liberation from that psychic trap has proved disappointingly difficult to achieve. In Chapters 2 and 3 we begin to look at more hidden factors, which first reveal themselves in the power-relations in those old institutions. Those power-relations look straightforward enough on the surface, but beneath we find a complicity of the weak. This view is developed in Chapter 4 to show how unconscious the complicity is, and how widespread in all sorts of relations within institutions. They gradually come into focus once we have become aware and sensitised to their occurrence.

Mobilisations of persons into emotional roles creates dramatisations which can be publicly visible. Dramatisations also contribute, as we shall see in Chapter 5, to serious communication problems within the institution. And in addition we can see how something we might call the institution's own thinking gets distorted and disconnected – even resulting in a fragmentation of thought resembling that in the mind of the psychotic patient. In Chapter 6 the incarceration in dysfunctional institutions promotes a revolt against it. The wish to overturn that institution, though on the surface rather adolescent, is in some respects a healthy reaction towards liberation from an unhealthy institutional climate. Such challenge may have deeply contradictory and paradoxical problems but it appears to be an irrepressible urge.

CHAPTER I

Reversing the Old Institutions

The shock I conveyed in the Prologue was widespread within psychiatry in the 1940s and 1950s when, after World War Two, the impetus for reconstruction and renewal was felt in the whole of society across Europe. The challenge for psychiatry was what to do with these old institutions.

Institutionalisation

One particularly perceptive account of the shock was given by the superintendent of Claybury Hospital in the medical journal *The Lancet*:

> ...the patient has ceased to rebel against, or to question the fitness of his position in a mental hospital; he has made a more or less total surrender to the institution's life... He is co-operative. Here 'co-operative' usually implies that the patient does as he is told with a minimum of questioning or opposition. This response on the part of the patient is very different from that of true co-operation essential to the success of any treatment, in which the patient strives to understand, and work with, the doctor in his efforts to cure... [The] patient, resigned and co-operative...too passive to present any problem of management, has in the process of necessity lost much of his individuality and initiative. (Martin 1955, pp.1188–1190)

By the 1950s many new ventures were started, though this is not the place to review them (see Clark 1965). Denis Martin's own hospital was on the way to becoming one of those (Martin 1955; Schoenberg 1972). These attempts early on (Clark 1964; Jones 1952; Mandelbrote 1965; Martin 1955) were led by charismatic doctors whose personalities resembled in some respect or other those of military leaders who could inspire men. They were hopeful times, referred to by David Clark as his 'nine exciting years' (Clark 1996). Looking back, we can now wonder if the common factor in all these various changes was the enthusiasm for, or devotion to, change itself by these inspired men in the post-war years of reconstruction.

However, revolution by exceptional and charismatic personalities was one thing, standard reform by ordinary doctors and nurses was quite different. Principles and models took over from creative inspiration (Manning 1989). And then the spirit often ran into the ground.

By the 1970s, and the period of my Prologue, there was despair again in the service. Various powerful pressures combined. The political pressure to enhance the economics of the NHS interacted with the enduring anxiety over the large mental hospitals, and new, more effective psychotropic medication. The belief that treatment required only a short stay within an institution was promoted on many fronts, and it seemed possible to close all the large mental hospitals. Enoch Powell, then Minister of Health, vowed in 1960 that he would in fact close them by 1970. This policy was grounded in the initial belief that it was possible to design quite different and wholly benevolent services that would be therapeutic. Hence was born the current phase of 'community care'.[1]

Simplistic solutions

Reactions against the old mental hospital were vigorous in the 1950s and 1960s. The reasoning took the following form: if the environment within the mental hospital visibly makes people worse, there must be an arrangement of the organisation which makes people better (or, at the least, does not make them worse). This required some thought about what ingredient of the old institutions made people worse: how does the social, institutional environment actually affect the individual's mental health? Unfortunately, as the idea of changing the institutions spread wider, the less sophisticated was the understanding of what change was necessary. Rather simplistic notions were introduced to change the old asylums, ones which were based mostly on naive alteration of the structure. If the problem was their *large size*, then they should be small units. If they were far from the communities they served, then the service should be rooted within the community instead. If it was, as Goffman described, their *total* – all day, all night – quality (Goffman 1968) then we could set up day hospitals; or in some places weekend hospitals, and night hospitals, where people could be treated when they are not at work. If there was no purposeful activity for patients, they should be organised in sheltered workshops. Or, if patients are locked up, then open the doors – a solution that only worked with the really powerful personalities in charge (later combined with the really powerful drugs, once they came in, in the late 1950s).

Other arguments were more politically motivated. In a period – the post-war period – when democracy was beginning its role as a significant motivator, then the re-distribution of power seemed the answer. If the problem was a hierarchy of power-relations between staff and patients, then these, too, could be changed to equality and to the empowering of patients. This required a considerable subtlety for those in charge, in order that they remain in charge, whilst also empowering patients. That subtlety of thought was not itself evenly distributed amongst medical superintendents and their staff, and could again lead to aberrant experiments in anarchy (e.g. Baron 1987).

In latter years, disappointments with these simple measures has grown in parallel to the increasing employment of the new institutions of 'community care'. Scepticism has increased because the phenomenon of institutionalisation has been found growing steadily again in small organisations, community care hostels for instance, or even day hospitals. Size, of itself, is not the key element we must tackle; nor the power-relations, as they appear; nor the overt relations with the community outside the institutions (Menzies 1988b [1989]), and so on (see Foster and Roberts 1998 for examples and summaries of many of these problems). Over the years and decades it has seemed that these measures were too simply formulated and the factors not sufficiently understood. There is now a literature on the shortcomings and inhumanity of the present alternative to the old institutions, the system of community care (Foster and Roberts 1998). This has contributed to the increasing disillusionment with the notion of 'community'.

With increasing media coverage, and therefore government anxiety, about the violently insane living in the 'community', we could be on the verge of a new change in policy, and the mushrooming of new 'secure accommodation'. If that is so, we are even more urgently in need of insightful understanding of the factors that turn institutions into inhumane ones, and wreak havoc on the integrity of the inmates. And thus we need more enquiry into the form that institutions must have in order to be potentially non-harmful (or even therapeutic). If we are to come up with any better results it will be because we attend to a 'deep' layer of functioning of those old mental health institutions. If we do not attend so, we will be in danger of walking blindly into further difficulties that are reminiscent of the past, and which we could avoid by more circumspection and respect for that past.

It would appear that new thinking has been, and is, needed to decide what a benevolent and therapeutic institution would be. The shock of the old mental hospitals led to a determination to close them, rather than learn from them. It side-stepped the important question: What *was* the problem with those old hospitals?

Note

1   See Busfield (1986) for an account of the development of this social policy; and Leff (1997).

CHAPTER 2

The Anxious Institution
and its Defensiveness

Why did the reversal of such straightforward characteristics as size, power-relations, 'totality' of the institution, purposelessness and so forth not turn out to be useful in the simple way expected? We must conclude that some rather deeper characteristics lie hidden behind the surface and visible phenomena which we sought to change.

Of course some obviously beneficial institutions have been created, but those institutions probably depended on special charismatic personalities to lead them, who could intuitively mitigate some of the unseen factors. One task must be to try to get a conscious leverage on those factors and not have to depend on the particularly intuitive personalities turning up at the right time and in the right place as if by accident.

If the search is on for a category of factors that are not so visible, the candidate I propose is that of unconscious processes. If so we must look for them in the unconscious layers of the individual human mind. We would then suppose that the distorting factors in the person's unconscious has detrimental effects on the institutions we create together.[1] That quality of unconsciousness can explain why these factors were understandably overlooked in the initial burst of enthusiasm for community care.

Therefore, the hypothesis is: aspects of the institution are significantly determined by unconscious functioning in the individuals who make up the institution. And a corollary is: if the difficulties lie outside conscious thinking in the realm of the unconscious unknown, can they be brought to conscious attention, not just by occasional intuition, but in a professional, reflective and potentially teachable form? This book develops these hypotheses, and reflects on the nature of the unconscious in institutions, those institutions for mental healthcare, and to some extent institutions in general.

We can start with the view that our minds relegate to the unconscious those experiences which cannot be borne. In mental health work we do indeed have to deal with impossible suffering. The individual's response is to put up psychological defences so as to remain unaware of the pain of the psychic work. I shall begin by looking at the way this, the structure of anxiety and defence in the individual, affects working in our institutions. Later, in Chapter 7, I will return to another aspect of the unconscious – the effects of the Oedipus complex on the way the institution is seen and then how it behaves. Here, I shall address the unconscious level in the institution that is connected with the fact that we must cope with high levels of intense personal anxiety and suffering.

Anxiety work

If living a human life creates anxieties of a degree of severity that is intolerable, then any conscious appreciation of those anxieties has to be resisted. It is then said to be 'defended against' and any awareness is relegated to a region beyond conscious knowledge. This is the anxiety/defence model used by psychoanalysts. It implies that there are states of mind, and of anxiety, which cannot be faced, and which therefore require specific methods for individuals to survive psychologically. There is a *prima facie* case for this being important in mental health, since the object of the work is in fact just those very desperate states of mind which have driven individuals to admission to our institutions.

In mental health work, staff are confronted with a particularly grave problem. By the time people come to a mental hospital they are at the end of the line. Our institutions are set up with the prime purpose of dealing with unwanted anxieties – they are unwanted by society, and so have to be continuously accepted from the community around us (Bott [1976] 1990). The inmates have exhausted the tolerance and ultimately all capacity their relatives have for withstanding the emotional burden. The protective resources of society have been overwhelmed and the mental health institution is expected to provide better. The psychiatric service is required to cope with those driven mad by their experiences, when no other persons can so cope. So, what kind of 'provision' is this which can tolerate the intolerable?

Thus, the particular work that is required of psychiatric staff is 'anxiety work'. It means coping with high levels of psychological tension, and it requires withstanding the intolerable. We must do first what the patient, his intimate relatives, or his friends and neighbours, and other professional helpers, cannot do – that is, to bear his experiences. This is a tall order, and it faces the service with the problem that staff must face unbearable suffering.

Staff confront those human anxieties as their job, but as human beings, they cannot be unaffected by the agony of others – their charges. To protect individuals from their suffering seems obviously to be humane. But we must help others whose psychic pain cannot be confronted. If an effective system means protecting the individuals from an intolerable intensity of anxiety, that must include staff as well as inmates. Inevitably this prompts psychological defences in individual staff members and it is now well known that these individual defences translate into specific organisational phenomena at the level of the institution. Unrealistic and maladaptive attitudes to the work arise and are held collectively to form the unconscious culture, and are expressed in specific ways in which the job is actually done in practice. Because these unconscious attitudes are maladaptive, the institution is rendered less competent (Hinshelwood and Skogstad 2000; Jaques 1953; Menzies 1959). Then other behaviour seems to click in, and will reduce the whole effectiveness of the system.

Our system needs to be examined from the point of view of these hidden and little discussed features of the unconscious culture. The professional system of caring strangers has to do better than the family and society the inmates come from, and in my view we can only really do this when we conceive our institution or service as a container – a sump even – for unbearable anxieties to drain into. Insofar as we lack this conception, our institutions fail in their task. The maladaptive institution flees from suffering, and in the process harms those within it. That is the deeper layer of institutions, which underlies those surface features first addressed when trying to deal with the old mental hospitals.

Cure and desocialisation

Explicitly the institution is set up to perform several tasks – typically: care, custody and cure. But inadvertently, it performs a fourth function – the institutionalisation of inmates. And to the list of the specific mental health tasks should be added: protecting vulnerable inmates from the system itself. Main (1946) expressed the problem in terms of a stability gained by retreating from intolerable experience, but at a price:

> [H]ealth and stability are often bought at the excessive price of desocialisation. Sooner or later the patient, alone and unsupported, must face the difficult task of returning to the society in which he

became unstable, and there again regain social integration and a daily sense of values and purpose. This task is no light one for a desocialised man. (Main [1946] 1989, pp.7–8)

So, in caring for patients with a mental illness in hospital, Main believed a kind of 'social illness' is substituted in the place of the mental illness. Patients develop a dependency on their doctors, their nurses and the system that flees from suffering. That dependence on the institution and its protective role in combating intolerable experiences leads to the inability to leave the institution.

One response is then to institute rehabilitation programmes to restore social skills to 'cured' individuals. But this is proceeding in piecemeal fashion. To restore the patient to being a full person again, we need to understand the deeper meaning of rehabilitation for him. The patient needs to cope once more with the intolerable experiences to which he was exposed in his family and friends before he came into hospital. By admission to the hospital, there is a tacit agreement to give him necessary respite. And whilst there, he tastes to some extent a system that can protect and defend him from the *internal* disaster inside himself. The hospital is a defensive system, despite its conscious intention to create cure and change with the benefits of pharmacology or therapy. When the patient returns to their old social setting where breakdown occurred, it is to a less effective defensive system, and indeed to a more anxious one. Dependency on the hospital as a better protection from himself leads, as we saw from the history of the mental hospitals, to permanently rising numbers of inmates. There the capacity to tolerate the intolerable was usually neglected in favour of more practical – externally oriented – forms of adaptation. Adaptation was *to the hospital*, with its unconscious protection. Then, less adapted to their home environment, they stay on, eventually clogging the service, with a declining quality of life, ending in institutions given over to demoralisation and despair.

That is what used to happen. Although it is now changed because long-term care in those institutions is no longer available, we can still understand that system, and recognise that any new system needs to plan on the basis of tolerating the intolerable. It must institute a system that deals with the anxieties and disturbance at conscious and unconscious levels in the individual.

Collective defences

The institution accepts disturbance and anxieties from outside and must continually provide a protective layer of some kind, against this inflow of disturbance. It would seem that we must continually adapt ourselves – our social structure – to cope with new patients, and to ensure they can cope with themselves.

In one sense, it is humane to protect patients 'against themselves' in this way. The problem is that the actual ways in which this occurs creates detrimental effects on those individuals as well. The defensive protection of the system against the intolerable suffering creates side-effects – the problem of institutionalisation.

Thus, one of the conclusions to this kind of thinking is that institutionalisation is not just an unfortunate side-effect of large institutions. The function which has institutionalisation as a side-effect also benefits individual persons, but in a specific way – it is a defensive benefit aimed at reducing awareness and thought about the core of the problem: the unbearable experience of suffering.[2]

The unconscious processes, which we have postulated are acting within the institution, may produce a benefit or detriment to the individuals. We must devote our interest and concern as much with the 'health' of the institution as with the health of the individuals. It is now clear that these two forms of health are connected in intricate ways. Proceeding with this hypothesis, we will turn in the next chapter to investigate this connection between individual and institution. It might be objected that the phenomena we need to get to grips with are unconscious – that is, outside of awareness – and therefore there will be no possibility of understanding them. This is wrong. Unconscious processes do reveal themselves, not least in their detrimental effects. So, their inner working is implicitly knowable by inference from their effects.

We began this chapter by asking why simplistic changes, based on reversing the characteristics of old institutions, have not had simple successes; and I have answered that the failing has been to overlook unconscious processes, particularly the hidden effects on the institution of its job of bearing the unbearable. This leads to questions, which we will now go into, about how those institutional processes result in the detrimental effects on the individual inmates.

Notes

1   See my previous work (Hinshelwood 1987a) for an earlier account of unconscious processes in institutions, upon which the present book builds.

2   Of course, institutionalisation is not solely found in mental health. It is at its height there, I believe, because the tensions and anxieties there are maximal. But many other working institutions provoke serious anxiety in their members, and embody collective defences for their relief, a prison for instance (Hinshelwood 1993a). But even fairly benign work, carried on in large institutions, has the effect of depersonalisation which comes from membership of a large collective (see Turquet, 1975, for an account of the identity problems of large group; and see Chapter 3).

Role-Relations
and Power-Relations

The last chapter introduced the idea that the institution itself provides collective protection against anxiety. How does it do so? Here we shall continue to explore that question by still probing what is known about those old institutions and to learn lessons from them. Vulnerable people lost important aspects of themselves as described in Martin's original description, given earlier (page 35). He claimed that personalities were distorted by the power-relations, and the patient lost his capacity to understand and to take part in his own treatment. Main described an unconscious defensive dimension in terms of the roles involved in healthcare. In a hospital, he says,

> only roles of health or illness are on offer; staff to be only healthy, knowledgeable, kind, powerful and active, and patients to be only ill, suffering, ignorant, passive, obedient and grateful. In most hospitals staff are there because they seek to care for others less able than themselves, while the patients hope to find others *more* able than themselves. The helpful and the helpless meet and put pressures on each other to act not only in realistic, but also phantastic collusion... [The] helpful will unconsciously *require* others to be helpless while the helpless will *require* others to be helpful. Staff and patients are thus inevitably to some extent creatures of each other. (Main 1975, p.61)

These phantastic others result in the patients being unrealistically helpless and the staff unrealistically helpful. Individuals lose their active and social selves, according to Martin (1955) and to Main (1946). If those institutions did give a certain degree of protection from psychic pain and anxiety, it was at the cost of distorting the identity of everybody who was embedded and moulded under the influence of those roles.

But Main's description gives an analysis of more specific unconscious dynamics. The individuals' personalities are split, and the unwanted is projected *into* the 'other' group. This begins a deeper understanding of processes which go on in damaging institutions. The patients lose their active selves, but staff are, unconsciously, driven to live up to phantasy images of being wholly powerful and knowledgeable. Both suffer in their different ways.

These descriptions are the beginnings of an understanding of how the institution can, in hidden ways, put pressure on the inmates' identities and potentially make them more 'ill' (or in the case of the staff, more 'well'). The recognition of this deleterious effect led Main (1946) and others to write in powerful terms against the institution. Their first initiative was to separate the illness from the effects of the social institution. Bierer (founder of the Marlborough Day Hospital in 1947) said in an interview with Richard Evans that there were two considerations:

> ...first, their (the patients') readjustment to themselves, second, their readjustment to the group, to society. Readjustment to themselves means integration of the 'ego', the 'id' and the 'superego'. Readjustment to the group means identification with the group without sacrificing too much of one's own personality. (Bierer and Evans 1969, p.47)

He was indicating two aspects to treatment – individual integration and social adaptation. So often, as Main conveys, they conflict with each other. However, Bierer indicated that the treatment of the individual can or should include social readjustment; and Main implied this too:

> ...a situation arises that reproduces the fundamental conflict between the individual and society...the individual is motivated by a desire to do well for himself, but by placing him in a situation where he can only operate through the medium of others, his spontaneous attitudes toward co-operation are revealed. (Main 1946, p.53)

Main directs our attention towards the social system as the place where the individual can recover his health. If this is so, we are directed towards understanding how he operates with his colleagues in developing a social system in which to have his symptoms, and get better from them.

Changing the medical culture

This kind of thinking, about the social system itself, began in the war-time effort in military psychiatry at Northfield Hospital in Birmingham, now Highcroft Hospital (Harrison 2000). Then, as always in war-time, the most radical experiments could be risked. In the 1940s, the question of how to learn from the old institutions came up and was furiously debated in that context. At Northfield, the notion of the purpose of the institution was debated; but questioning the purpose had direct influence on the way the hospital culture developed.

One possible purpose of the military hospital is, perhaps, that the army needs functioning units of soldiers. The unit has to function; and its health must be measured. It is measured in terms of morale – a social measure. There, at Northfield, more than any civilian hospital, they had to take account of the social health. Under the influence of John Rickman, Wilfred Bion experimented with the Rehabilitation Wing in these terms:

> In the treatment of the individual, neurosis is displayed as a problem of the individual. In the treatment of the group it must be displayed as a problem of the group. (Bion and Rickman 1943, p.678)

He enlisted army thinking and sought to engage his soldiers in a collaboration with him over how to deal with the problems of his Wing. He stressed lethargy, purposelessness and loss of pride as the general features of low morale, and thus the manifestations of a general 'neurosis' of the whole group of men in the Wing. Thinking in military terms, he claimed they needed an enemy – and that was neurosis. They needed, too, an experienced leader to lead them in the battle against it – and that leader would be himself.[1] He required them to think about the enemy – neurosis – and to fight it. The weapon he asked them to use was to think about their state as a fighting unit, and make suggestions for improving things. Various activities, clubs and group functions were suggested by the men and instituted, to the general improvement of the morale and atmosphere of the Wing. This approach to the unit was successful in a military sense.

However, Bion had created a contest between the medical culture, which focused on the individual exclusively, and his new culture, organised around a set of ideas about the mutual impact of the individual and his social environment on each other (Hinshelwood 1999c). In effect, he had replaced a normal hospital environment, focused on the individual's malady, with a military one in which the individual, in practice expendable, was deployed for the purpose of the battle unit, whose condition was the first priority of its leader. Bion claimed that his culture was more appropriate for rehabilitation back to the army.

It is common-sense that putting a collection of neurotic individuals with apparently inexplicable difficulties together will result in a group with inexplicable difficulties. But, it was a unique approach to address the morale of the unit – rather than the patients. In those early days, that approach challenged the notion of a hospital, and in fact it did create an initially hostile reaction at Northfield. Added to that it severely disconcerted the military authorities who had responsibility for the hospital if doctors 'played at' being military men! Bion was removed from duties at Northfield and moved elsewhere.

Nevertheless it is an important experiment, and though it did not succeed in the long term, it too has lessons for us. Main (1977) criticised Bion for neglecting to inform and reassure the superordinate levels of the military hierarchy and medical authorities of the hospital, who were disconcerted by this experiment. This neglect is often thought to be a warning lesson and instructs us in the application of systems theory to attend to *all* levels in an organisation. But my concern is different. It is with the specific cultural issues that Bion was struggling with and to the details of the anxieties that Bion was dealing with. Thus, we need to pay attention not only to the formal aspects of a system, and its levels, but to its emotional functioning as an institution. By dismantling one culture, the medical one, he appeared to release anxieties. They were expressed in the criticism that he had reneged on his medical and military duties. The doctors thought he abandoned the care of individual patients. The military authorities thought he brought indiscipline.[2] In turn, those anxieties he provoked destroyed his experiment.

Despite the disgrace it brought upon the experimenter, this approach betrayed a more sophisticated approach to an institution. His idea was to tackle aspects of the culture (not the individual) – the belief system about its structure and function: what kind of leadership, what enemy, and how it should be approached. Bion (and Rickman) attempted to replace one culture with another, one kind of authority (medical) with another (military). However, though this radical change is in the right direction for our purposes, it contrasts with the approach I am discussing, in which we attempt to *investigate* the culture, not just change it.

Analysis of power

Main was also at Northfield, arriving in the wake of Bion's experiments, but profoundly influenced by that legacy. He became aware of the dichotomy between focusing on the individual *versus* focusing on the social unit – and, like Bion, was persuaded of the need for a different kind of authority. However, he was more judicious in trying to deal with the actual hospital authorities (Main 1977). His focus was not on choosing which culture, but on the dichotomous relations between the two.

As we recognised earlier, Main saw that power-relations involved the power to make projections, projecting the more passive traits of character into the patient. In the quote above (page 46) he described the psychodynamic interchange between the two sub-groups, and emphasised the psychological level of polarisation between dominance and passivity. He saw these features as diverging into a dichotomy. Different aspects of personality became different persons – the helpless and the helpful.

In an extreme degree this is described luridly by Cooper, who likened the authority within psychiatry to that within a Nazi extermination camp:

> By domination of the other the leader produces for himself the illusion that his own internal organisation is more and more perfectly ordered. The Nazi extermination camps were one product of the Dream of Perfection. The Mental Hospital, along with many other institutions in our Society, is another. In the camp bodily existences were systematically annihilated, each body containing, in terms of the illusion, the projected badness, sexual anomaly, meanness of the camp officials and the society they represented. This murder was always ritual murder aimed at the purification of the murderer and it was essentially a manner of evading guilt. (Cooper 1967, pp.96–97)

This gives an analysis of the defensive needs of persons in authority to escape from the anxieties of their own bad impulses. In the mental hospital, passivity and weakness (as well as madness) are projected entirely into the patients, and that allows the authorities a defensive escape from their own weakness. This conveys a view that all authority and power are bad. And many of the developments in many institutions, including therapeutic communities, in the 1960s drew their vitality from that analysis.

The view is a Foucaultian one, in which professional status carries with it the privilege of wielding that status as a dominance over others. With regard to the medical profession, it is to imprint the power of doctors upon the bodies of its patients; or, within psychiatry, to imprint the power of the psychiatric professions upon the minds of their helpless patients.

However, latterly, difficulties over authority in the professions, and increasing contests over power and status have gained momentum. Rivalrous professions – nurses, doctors, psychologists, social workers – may claim 'to be only healthy, knowledgeable, kind, powerful and active' through competitive projections into the helpless patients (page 45).

Moreover, patients fear their active selves, it seems (see Donati 1989), because of the neurotic or mad manifestations. Then they introject the characteristic passive aspects of personality projected by the staff, and exaggerate their own. In due course, they project their active selves into the staff. That fearful side of themselves is attributed to staff and feared therein. Together, as Main said, they become 'creatures of each other'. Because patients make counter-projections, Cooper seems to have over-stated his case against professional authorities. He fails to acknowledge a kind of psychological complicity by the patients with the professionals. Thus, the power-relations that appear on the psychological surface seem one-sided.

Main's description is a resolutely two-way system of unconscious dynamics that creates the social roles into which the individuals must fit, at the instigation of both. Both are 'creatures of each other' (page 45). Both sides – staff and patients – are reduced to one-dimensional characters. Both sides induce staff to be caricatures of power and both induce the patients' role to be a caricature of weakness.

Sometimes this kind of description is erroneously believed to put responsibility on victims, and exonerate those professionals who exploit and persecute. This is not a conclusion to be drawn. Those with formal authority retain responsibility. It is just that their responsibility should include the system which institutes this kind of projective system of power and weakness (Hinshelwood 1997a); and they should make use of the available knowledge of such mutual projective systems, which is now available.

Thus, Main implies complex relations underpinning powerful authorities, and this play of power and authority re-casts the nature of institutionalisation, our starting point. The apparent potential for power to rest with a class in authority – in this case, the staff – is obvious, on the surface. However, beneath the surface the power of the staff rests upon subtle psychological dynamics, played out by both sides. These are not easily discerned, but they direct, sustain, and transmit to future institutional members, the redistribution of power – and of weakness. They do not do it without the 'active' complicity of the 'weak' patients. Both sides are active in creating this division. Both are active in separating activity from passivity. Both are powerful at separating power from weakness.

We need to be aware of this hidden subtlety and the power of the projections that are involved in projecting power. Thus, a central and profoundly interesting fact is that such groups do not lack cohesion. In appearance there is a clear division, a hiatus, a fault-line between powerful active authority and a weak, passive and dominated undergroup. But behind that appearance of fracture is a system based on a complicity of *both* groups to engage in this redistribution of their personality characteristics. Together they create a particular quality of visible power-relations, which can resemble those of a concentration camp, however well-meaning the participants were when they entered the system with their conscious intentions (see also Hinshelwood 1997a for an extended treatment of this personality-distorting form of coercive influencing of people). The inmates of institutions (staff and patients combined) do not have difficulties in co-operation over some functions; a large mental hospital is evidently superbly effective as an institutionalising machine. There is co-operation on all levels in the function of institutionalising new members.

We have needed to clarify the social relations within the institutions – and to have a way of gaining access to their unconscious dimensions and meanings. It is, thus, more than a problem of the individual. We conclude this chapter with the understanding that relations within an institution suffer under the pressures of distorting conditions. We must ask the question: how do we spot these distortions going on at the less visible and unconscious levels beneath the surface? We need to begin to think about how individuals do, in practice, collaborate together, and in particular how we spot such collaboration. And we will proceed to this in the next chapter.

Notes

1   Bion had, in fact, led a tank battalion into battle in World War One.

2   Indeed requiring the ordinary private to engage in considering the problems for himself must have seemed a distinctly unmilitary approach.

CHAPTER 4

The Community Personality
Complicity and Dramatisation

We have discovered that the culture the individual is part of has effects on him, and thus that culture should itself be a part of the therapeutic investigation. Equally, that cultural system is in some ways the product of those who make it up – all of them. And they in their role-behaviour and role relationships reconstitute it every day.

Moreover, we are prompted to address not just the pathology of the social system itself, but the individual's complicity within it. We must study the forms of belonging that the individual person makes to his community, and thus the contribution he makes to the social medium in which he belongs. Hidden aspects of an organisation give benefit to both sides of this system.

How then is an individual complicit in the social 'pathology' of the institution? We need a method to give us leverage on that defensive social system that grows up around the individuals.

Cultural 'fits'

I shall start with why these mutual psychodynamics occur. Although this will be elaborated in later chapters, it is worth giving a brief account in general terms. Based on the original notion of defence against some intolerable experience, we can understand the two separate motivations of the two halves of a hospital community.

Cooper gave a one-sided description of the authorities in a mental hospital projecting into the inmates certain 'bad' aspects of their own personalities (page 49). This is one-sided. But we need a description of the other side as well. Rosenberg (1970) reported the patients' sets of attitudes to the staff:

[T]he hospital sub-culture provides a setting in which a number of people can share a common system of ego defences in a way that simultaneously helps to reduce intrapsychic tensions while permitting the maintenance of a stable institutional structure. Furthermore it will be argued that this relationship is far from fortuitous. That is, I shall hypothesise that the defensive needs and intrapsychic conflicts common to much of the patient population constitutes a base line around which the institutional structure has evolved. (Rosenberg 1970, p.23)

And in detail:

Patients' ambivalence about dependency needs may be handled in several ways. The central-defensive myth of the patient culture portrays the inmates as persons who, due to circumstances beyond their control, have been put in a place where they don't want to be and should not be... What is not dealt with in the explanatory system of the patient culture, or in those of its observers, is the possibility that certain persons may have motivational sets which make them amenable to coercion and which may make external control and degradation gratifying. By portraying himself as powerless, a patient can rationalise every act and feeling, that he experiences, as being the resultant of coercion rather than an expression of his own self. The degree to which this explanation is ingrained in the patient culture reinforces the feeling that it might be described as collective repression and projection... [T]he wish to be controlled is transformed into the cultural belief that the institution is unduly repressive. The possibility of regressing to a relationship which approaches the father–child or mother–child prototype is so minimal as to be functionally non-existent. Thus the individual is free from the possibility of acting out his regressive phantasies and need not suffer the anxiety that would accompany the attempt to ward off this movement... Furthermore, the hostile aspects of the ambivalence toward authority can be easily maintained since the rewards provided, although gratifying, still fall far short of generosity. Indeed the condescending manipulation through the use of petty rewards is a sound basis for justifying true rage. (pp.31–32)

This reports a set of collective, defensive attitudes involved in the patients' accepting the helpless, passive and dependent role described by Main. Rosenberg's account is, in a way, unfair in giving responsibility for the projective initiative to patients, driven by their own ambivalence and suffering. Like Cooper, Rosenberg is one-sided – but in the opposite direction. Nevertheless, together they can describe a coherent system in which both sides entwine around each other in a mutual complicity. Cooper described the projection by staff authorities of bad or mad impulses into patients; Rosenberg's patients projected their dependent wish as the staff's need to control. Thus, the defensive needs of two groups of people interlock neatly to form an extremely stable social system. Each is occupied by a different 'defensive myth', as Rosenberg calls it, by which each achieves a stable, mutual misunderstanding of each other. Each side sees the other in distorted form.

Both sub-group cultures endure because the identities that are constructed by the projective system offer the individuals some advantage. We conclude therefore that institutionalisation is a collaborative social function which may provide benefits for individual persons, a way in which people can help each other – the helpless to find exaggeratedly powerful help, and the helpful to fulfil a swollen ambition of helpfulness. It is not just an unfortunate side-effect of large institutions. This dynamic is the core of the means by which the unbearable is borne. It serves a specific purpose which must be served, in some way or other, healthily or unhealthily.

Dramatisation and negotiation

The individuals' role in this process of invitation or coercion into the group dramatisation is problematic (documented in exhaustive detail by Turquet 1975).

Despite descriptions of these institutional dynamics, they take place at the level of individuals interacting – and agreeing, in some implicit way, to interact – and to express something that is group-wide. The following illustration describes individuals (one in particular) negotiating to express something about the way that therapy in the community was perceived during a certain period. That patient's own preoccupations seem utterly self-centred. But she could eventually draw in others to enact a scene in the community meeting – a dramatisation. So, from a different point of view – which sees the individual complicit in the wider social group – she demonstrated the collective myth of a moralising therapist in a scene which the rest of the community, staff and patients, were absorbed by. (This illustration was previously published in Hinshelwood 1987a, pp.51–52.)

> In a community meeting in a day hospital, Ellen changed from being a
> leader of a practical discussion on hospital organization to become the

sad victim of an unwarranted attack which had happened the previous night. At the time she was staying in the small in-patient unit. This unit of a half-a-dozen beds provided accommodation for day patients in crisis whilst in the community of 30–40 patients. She had come back for supper with two men who were day patients, not resident in that unit. The day patients were not entitled to supper and Ellen was 'attacked' by the night nurse.

Apparently she was told off again by Susan, the nurse who was in charge the following morning. Susan, who was present at the meeting, gave a less harsh version of the occurrence.

It seems that Ellen had not in fact known these regulations since she had been living in the unit for only two days. Ellen took on the role of innocent victim unjustly condemned. She cried and cried and implored Susan not to criticise her so. For Susan, it had been necessary to explain the supper regulations to Ellen. Yet everything Susan said, by way of explanation, Ellen took as searing criticism and responded to with wounded crying.

The meeting gained momentum faced with Ellen's tortured responses. A righteous indignation against the night nurse now developed as many were moved by Ellen's sobs. She was pictured as neurotically unfit for her job. Ellen remained tearfully hurt and it appeared nearly impossible to focus attention on her own role in all this.

Had she in some masochistic way attracted an attack upon herself? She was indeed at the moment suffering under what she believed were continuing attacks from Susan. Ellen skilfully countered any attempt to look into her own potential for fitting into a victim role – cowering away from the group into her tears, as if the meeting was pursuing the same attack. Eventually a crisply impatient member actually 'gratified' Ellen by taking up the role of harsh inquisitor, and the meeting polarised for or against her.

Ellen felt a chillingly vicious attack of blame and condemnation. It was however quite remote from other people's experience of what had gone on. Ellen's version came from her own internal world of experience, in which she was prone to writhe under the flagellation of an internal persecution. Externalising this conscience neutralised it by discrediting it.

The example shows how an internal 'bad conscience' was cloaked by enrolling external participants. The internal sources of such situations were then denied, and the external provocations acknowledged in order to gain external support to discredit the persecutor. The world of actual external relations can often provide very convincing justifications. This does not deny that she could, at times, adapt well to the external world of the community. At this very meeting she had effectively led a discussion about important community issues. That leadership potential also enabled her to co-ordinate others in dramatising her own internal relationship (the accusatory persecution) in the arena of the external relationships in the meeting.

The individual – in this case, Ellen – was drawn into a focal position. She did not refuse it; and she was, in a significant way, complicit in achieving her experience of being accused and punished. First, it was the nurse Susan, but because Susan was resistant to playing the part of persecutor actually in the meeting – and other staff supported Susan's resistance – another had to be found; this was another patient member. Negotiation to find recruits for the parts to be dramatised is wholly implicit, and unconscious.

Isolation and dramatisation

The individual often feels alone in his lonely stand to be himself.[1] But that aloneness can itself be recruited in certain suitable individuals. They are alone in the context of mutual fitting-in with others in the dramatisation of the community. The following illustration is again the community meeting of a therapeutic community and I shall indicate how it is a set of staff–patient relationships which form a collective (paranoid) defence against the fear in the community at the time, of being let down or abandoned (this illustration was previous published in Hinshelwood 1979a, pp.110–112). The particular personality resources of the individual can come to the fore and be 'latched onto' by others in this process of collectivisation.

> In a mid-week meeting, one of the more dominant members, A, came into the room with two walking sticks and her leg in plaster. She sat down and asked another member to put a chair under her leg. She was thus very prominent and was the single focus of attention for the group during the first half hour or so. The meeting was in effect A's own monologue. Such a monologue had been a feature of community meetings for some time and A, having a talent for it, often took the role.

The staff had become generally doubtful that such a meeting, dominated by a monologue, was a valuable one. They often puzzled about what could be done about it.

As on other occasions, after some twenty minutes or so the monologue was interrupted by a member of staff, X, who remarked on the manner of presentation adopted by the patient in this meeting. It is necessary to convey a brief impression of A. Her admission to the community followed her separation from a much loved lesbian partner with whom she had lived for some thirty years. A's behaviour in the community had been violent and provocative of violence, which seemed to be both sadomasochistic and also abreactive. Her disinhibited behaviour was regularly assisted by heavy drinking before meetings. At the meeting I am reporting, X, the member of staff, had been struck by a lessening of her violence and provocativeness. He guessed that she had not been drinking so much and related his own impression that she was easier to empathise with, to the fact that she was not drunk. X confided all this to A and to the meeting. A's response, in her masochistic way, was to insist that this was a moral condemnation of her drinking. X protested that, if anything, he had been trying to convey a note of approval. But interestingly, the note of condemnation was claimed also by two or three others (who happened to be heavy drinkers, too). They confirmed that A was being criticised. Clearly there was some seriously entrenched misperception; possibly a quite delusional state of affairs arising.

Though there had been a slight movement away from the monologue, the meeting could not be said to have changed for the better. For the staff, the meeting gave a feeling of being still trapped in some unproductive state. This state in which A was being condemned and X was being stubbornly misperceived is one indication of a collective defence operating. The meeting, when it did become a dialogue, did not take up A's point about her loneliness and feeling of rejection, but became a set of antipathetic relations between patients and staff. A was still left alone with her loneliness.

The dislocation in the communication between, on one hand, X, representing staff, and, on the other, a vocal group of the patient members seemed to express the collective view that a hoped-for sympathetic listener had been lost and was replaced by a monstrously critical judge. Staff X had become trapped in this. He had become the embodiment of that judge. In this meeting the staff expressed in themselves (with X as spokesman) the task simply of stopping the monologue. Such a reflex strategy seemed fixed on the view that merely to stop something unproductive would reveal and liberate something productive. But that entailed a problem – the contradiction of interrupting the monologue while at the same time wanting to appear to listen as psychotherapeutic professionals. The meeting continued.

> Later Y, another member of staff, made a different intervention. It seemed to Y that although X's remark had not been successful, it was substantially accurate. Y took it up and remarked that, although A was easier to empathise with and although most other people must have suffered similar experiences to the ones of loss that she had been talking about in her monologue, in fact nobody was able to say so, or to share their own experiences with A. This was responded to by a couple of members agreeing that they had experienced similar separations from loved ones. This led into attacks on certain members of the nursing staff who were thought to lack understanding, criticism of them in general over confusing changes in the timetable, and then to a brief reminiscence about a popular and sympathetic occupational therapist who had left the hospital the previous week.

That seemed more successful; at least, more people joined in and more community issues were raised. Y had drawn attention to a communication problem in the meeting and connected it with the experience of loneliness and loss. A definite movement took place – from the monologue to a more widespread but explicit expression of the feelings of separation and of having no one who understands. Some kind of recognition of this separation and aloneness enabled members to come together hesitantly in a dialogue with each other and with staff about the sense of isolation.

The monologue pattern demonstrated this isolation in a dramatic way rather than in a verbal way; it was a dramatisation, an indication of a collective set of attitudes. The intervention of Y had catalysed a move from the unconscious dramatisation to a more conscious awareness that could be expressed. The point about this meeting is the expression in dramatic form of certain collective attitudes (about loss). That defensiveness, the sense of criticism and confrontation, later moved towards a conscious reflection on losing someone (a member of staff in the here-and-now).

Although A's loneliness was displayed on the surface in her monologue, and left her isolated with her feelings, beneath the surface there was a complicity by all to engage with A in demonstrating a lonely monologue. But in that demonstration one can see the hidden collective intermeshing, that could betray the loneliness and reveal the collective defences. In the final moments of the meeting, when loss and loneliness were discussed, the group displayed in a more overt, honest and healthy way that the individuals could come together in the experience of loneliness. We could make the hypothesis that the move from dramatisation to reflection is the core of a healthy institution.

The more useful intervention was not about A's own mental state, but about her manifest role to represent, or dramatise, the isolation and lack of rapport *actually at the moment within the meeting*. The subsequent discussion showed deep and general feelings about members of staff, anger at being abandoned or excluded, and envy that resulted in criticism and denigration of the nurses. The feeling of being let down and unsupported was indicated at multiple levels – including the fractured leg. The message was that the community felt not properly articulated – or, in effect, fractured.

In fact, this meeting took place just prior to the summer period, when many members and staff were about to go away on holiday. The experience of what this meant was hinted at in the apparent inability of A to get any response or to share experiences with the community. The community could not share her loss and heartbreak, but gave an initial opportunity to create a paranoid situation – between patients and staff – as a diversion from the individual aloneness, whilst expressing it.

Collaboration and communication

There is here a highly complex picture. Manifestly there is an irritating occurrence in which one member of the meeting appears to abolish all reasonable communication. At a different level, this irritation has a quite different meaning; it is a collaborative dramatisation of situations in which many people felt isolated by the excluding kind of experience which the hospital at the time engendered.

This form of collaboration, I claim, is similar to that discovered in Main's description of institutionalisation, when the helpless and the helpful push each other to extremes, and become 'creatures of each other'. So, the isolated one and the 'isolators' push each other into those positions. There is an elaborate reverberation between the individual and the community environment about feeling linked in, about belonging, and about being understood – or, rather, the negatives of these. Here both an individual – the one who I call the monologist – and the community collaboratively enact their experience. It is not consciously contrived, and was perhaps only half-grasped too by the staff.

These illustrations demonstrate the potential visibility of these projection systems. But we can now ask if these occurrences are merely curiosities, just epiphenomena in institutions with rather odd people. Can these observations point to the more obvious problems of institutions in general?

Note

1   Psychotics give up that stand, since they have such a weak existential sense of themselves.

CHAPTER 5

Communication
Linking and Thinking

The question addressed in the last chapter was how to make these hidden dynamics more transparent. The evidence of the illustrations was that un-conscious collaboration, as illustrated, where something goes on outside anyone's ken, leads to these dramatisations. Some better conscious awareness of these distorting and collusive arrangements seemed to liberate the institution from the driven quality of the unconscious.

But what other institutional consequences occur? I will describe two important features of organisations where these hidden (but imprisoning) dynamics operate more generally: distorted communication and frag-mented thinking.

Boundaries and barriers

Jaques (1951) described the variability of communication between sub-groups within an organisation. There is less communication between members of different sub-groups than between members of the same group. Communication within groups is different from, and more extensive than, communication between groups, but this is not necessar-ily problematic for the organisation. For example, communication is limited between myself, a doctor, and the porter. I don't think my utter-ances couched in psychiatric jargon would be useful to his knowledge of the central heating system. His knowledge of the organisation of the kitchen are a mystery for me. Nor is it *necessary* for us to reach mutual un-derstanding on these topics. What is essential is that there should be the *opportunity* for open communication between us when there are matters of mutual concern; for instance, if we have to discuss how to ensure the boiler room is out-of-bounds for unauthorised members of the community. This is communication on a 'need-to-know' basis. Communication is restricted, but it is a functional restriction on communication. When, however, there are barriers to communication about matters that *are* of mutual concern – when the need-to-know system fails – we have a different situation, a damaging one. And then we suspect a defensiveness hidden in the cultural attitudes and projections.

There is an important distinction here between two kinds of restricted communication. Following Jaques (1951), the first, 'adaptive segregation', is the useful restriction of communication in a complex organisation when groups of individuals communicate freely with each other as necessary – and do not over-burden each other with excess information exchanges. The second, he called 'maladaptive segmentation'. In those instances the restrictions are not to do with matters of efficiency and need. Instead they result from projections into other groups of certain disowned aspects of the individual in the index group, who are then disadvantaged in listening correctly to what the other group communicated. Instead, the index group 'interprets' the communication in terms of the (usually bad) qualities that they project into the others. This is in line with the examples of Cooper and of Rosenberg given above, and of those from my own examples.

Jaques' phrases – 'adaptive segregation' and 'maladaptive segmentation' – are cumbersome, and I have referred simply to 'boundaries' and 'barriers' (Hinshelwood 1979a). The maladaptive kind, a barrier, may not only be a lessening of communications, but also a distortion of communications, an example of which comes next.

Distorted communication

The powerful, but implicit, factors operating on the communication processes render communication very different from what we ordinarily mean by the word – something in which clear and conscious meanings are transferred from one person to another. Incidentally, we might suggest as a general proposition that mental ill-health is a tendency for the proportion of collaborative distortion to predominate over communication proper. It is worth examining some of the specific forms bad communication takes, since it is again an indicator of something hidden. It is a useful alerting pointer to hidden dynamics. That move from communication towards collaborative enactment is conveyed in an illustration given by David Cooper.

> Nowhere were anxieties more evident than in the highly significant distortions of the hospital communication process... A typical incident

processed by the communication system was the following: a young man in the unit [for male schizophrenic patients, and run as a therapeutic community] had a girl-friend in a female ward; one night she became hysterically upset about an issue connected with her ward and treatment, and he and a friend attempted to console her and help her back to her ward; she noisily resisted these attempts and a member of the portering staff who witnessed the incident called a nurse who took her back to her ward. The porter informed the night nursing superintendent, who informed the unit and reported to the day nursing administration, who reported finally to the divisional meeting. The final version was that two male patients from the unit had attacked a female patient and, it was implied, were attempting to carry her off for sexual purposes. The phantasy existing in the minds of many staff outside the unit is that rape, sexual orgies and murder are daily occurrences in the unit. (Cooper 1967, p.99)

Here the communication displays the development of emotionally toned distortions in the identities of whole groups within the hospital. The hospital in this example seemed to use the unit as a receptacle for unwanted aspects of their own individuals' identities, just as the helpful use the helpless as receptacles for their disowned helplessness. A true 'barrier' was erected around the unit. The minds of individuals in the hospital located the disowned aspects of identity – unruly sexuality and aggression in the unit. Distorted communication involves the radical reconstruction of a person's sense of identity, for recruitment into a dramatisation where specific emotional attitudes and prejudices ferment. Accurate communication succumbs to these group-induced emotional states of mind.

Within those sub-groups, separated by communication *barriers*, sets of beliefs arise about other groups, and those beliefs are maintained without adequate testing. These are cultural phenomena, and the shared attitudes confined within barriers amount to a belief system, or a myth. Communication problems across barriers show up in contrasting attitudes on either side of the boundary. These attitudes, though contrasted, also 'fit' with each other in a stable dissonance, as we discussed above (pages 52–54). Those groups who mutually misperceive each other are linked closely together. The link is not a straightforward one for passing information backwards and forwards in pursuit of working on the task of the organisation. Quite differently the link is in the form of projections which are passed back and forth between the groups in pursuit of an emotional peace of mind. They lead to quite different interpretations of events, and that hampers realistic dialogue, since communication is then devoted to sustaining distorted perceptions and identities. In the mental hospital, for example, staff will say to themselves 'these people behave irresponsibly, so for their own good we will lock the doors' (or 'give Largactil injections' etc.); patients may say to themselves 'the staff are critical and punitive and therefore they lock us up like prisoners'. Such disparate attitudes and underlying assumptions make communication leading to co-operation, thinking and decision-making impossible and sustain the existence of an unacknowledged underlife (Goffman 1968), as both sides believe they have confirmation of their misperceptions.

Induced roles (and identities) for the individuals are specific features of the collaboration between individuals in an institution where emotional barriers to communication occur.

Fragmented thinking

Moving now to the second major form of distortion, it is not just communication links between persons and groups which fail. Links fail to be made (or to persist) between ideas, or between the thoughts people have and the reality about which those thoughts speak. I will use the work of Sheena Grunberg (1979)[1] on thinking in the therapeutic community to illustrate this.

The therapeutic community has become an example of a reflective practice, as currently conceived: 'We have reached the point of a thinking community, where the structure supports the whole group reflecting upon itself' (Grunberg 1979, p.257). In a way the therapeutic community can, like a person, be said to have a 'personality' that can think, feel, disintegrate etc. (see also Stapley 1996).

Thinking, notably about the community itself, is the first casualty of tension and pathology in an organisation. At times, it can be located more or less solely within the members of staff. Then, the community meetings of a therapeutic community need to set about spreading the thinking function more evenly across the community. Such work is now referred to as reflective practice (and it may also take the form of action research in other institutions). In Grunberg's case study, the therapeutic community was divided, not so much into helpers and helpless, but between those who thought and those whose minds were empty of thinking. Grunberg described progressive steps taken by the therapeutic community to tackle this divide. She described the evolving structure of a large community meeting over a three-year period (I summarise her description).

Phase I: For some time, the community meeting had been characterised by a heavy atmosphere with the main communication coming from staff, or from certain 'leading' patients imitating staff. Interpretations about the group often either fell flat, or were received with sullen silence or even actively resisted, individual interpretations being found much more acceptable (described in detail in Hinshelwood and Grunberg 1979). The sense of real community was often at a low ebb. The large group was depleted and seemed to fragment. More and more of the community personality was split off from the community meetings. Energy was devoted instead to proliferation of other groups, none of which linked with, or bore any relation to, each other. Treatment in this piecemeal fashion made it hard to justify the community meetings.

Staff found it a great relief to get into their post-meeting group after the community meeting. There they could let go of their feelings, initially with a release of tension by laughter, heated discussions, smoking and the hugging of coffee cups. They regained projected parts of themselves and restored their own identity after the emotional draining. An attempt was made to think about the large group, whilst dispersed patients met in the kitchen and obviously had the need to do the same.

The fragmentation of the community personality had its counterpart in the staff meetings. After the initial relief of tension, a different tone came upon the staff group. It was noticeable that as one person's version of reality conflicted with another, strife emerged. Each defended their perception as the 'right' one. Any richness from bringing differing points of view together was lost. Different aspects of the feeling brought from the community meeting were projected into staff members, and then isolated there. This structure evaded linking with each other, and so allowed no proper constructive thinking to take place. That impairment of thinking could compare with the corruption and destruction of links between sub-groups, in the earlier part of this chapter.

Phase II: A process of modification was then embarked upon. A feedback of 15 minutes at the start of community meetings was instituted to bring in the knowledge of, and thinking about, the isolated, but lively, peripheral groups. The staff meeting afterwards allotted two places to patient representatives in the post-meeting group, in order to link separated parts of the community.

However, this failed. It was gradually overtaken by another stultifying routine. In this case, bland and endless reportage in the feedback section of the community meeting took over. Staff meetings became dulled as they could no longer restore themselves by abreacting emotions that had filled staff in the community meeting.

Phase III: Increasingly patients exerted pressure on the staff to change the system again. It was felt that it was easier to think in a smaller group, so the staff believed a 'fish-bowl' structure might be the answer. To tackle active staff and passive patients the post-group staff meeting was organised to take place as a fish-bowl; any patients who wished, remained in an outer circle to 'observe'. This structure was adopted to make a bridge for thinking about the community as a whole, to be heard not just by the staff but the whole community. At first, it was decided that no one in the outer group was obliged to attend and they were not allowed to speak. This was later modified to the point where the outer ring was allowed to speak after a quarter of an hour and then, finally, no time limit was imposed.

These modifications were controlled by the staff who in effect continued to hold the functions of thinking and deciding. But this, too, failed. The atmosphere in the staff meeting, held in concentric circles and therefore under observation, was very intense, thinking was serious, no laughs and jokes of the old staff meeting. The outer circle of patients was poorly attended and supine, 'clandestine conversations took place behind hands, reading of newspapers and an occasional vigilante sitting bolt upright listening to the endless intellectualisation' (Grunberg 1979, p.254).

The evolution of the structure had served only to create a clearer and clearer dramatisation. The polarising projections created ever more visibly thinking staff and ever more passive patients. The concentric circles exemplified a distorted solution reached when the thinking only involved a section of the community. At the time, it was done in all good faith, but it clearly served the staff's need to control. It did however make the fault-line in the community personality more visible.

Phase IV: Then,

> One particular morning the inner circle was debating about two
> significant events which had been raised in the large meeting, and
> inevitably, an erudite discussion about the relation to the two breasts
> resulted. This revelation met with nodded approval by the inner circle,

but was blasted by an illegal and outraged voice from that lone vigilante, who cried out: 'two ears – two eyes – two hands – two legs – TWO FEET!' Here was a plea for the community feet to be firmly placed on the communal floor. This was the beginning of a new upsurge of the demand for participation. (Grunberg 1979, p.254)

One of the severe criticisms by the patients at this time was of being asked to play out empty roles in the community, and in the work groups particularly. The gagging of the patient group was, not surprisingly, felt as a controlling political repression.

During all the changes in the community meeting in the first three phases, increased patient participation was developing in other functions of the community. It was particularly notable in the policy and assessment groups which, prior to this time, had consisted of staff alone with patient representatives. Also during that time there was a collapse of the work groups, with abandonment of gardening, repairing toys, painting old people's houses, etc. Work was considered empty and peripheral to what was considered to be the actual work task of the community. The inclusion of the patients in the assessment group (for new referrals) despite some ethical problems, and in the policy meeting, gave some patients a real say in the making of their own destiny.

The concentric circle function gradually became redundant, partly due to its stale quality, but also because the thinking function was being given back elsewhere. As part of this more equable distribution of health, ten half-hour sessions of the whole community were allocated to the discussion of the structure itself. They examined the concentric circles arrangement with a view to organising a structure to facilitate greater integration. At the end of these studies, a final decision was reached jointly. The post-community meeting was attended by all the community with the task specifically now of thinking about the community itself.

From then on, a different quality of interaction and participation occurred. Patients themselves learned some real group understanding and could develop their own skill in commenting on it, rather than by imitation. An apt interpretation brought about a palpable closeness in the community and a greater capacity for acknowledging the experience of others. There was also a change in the character of decision-making in the community. Instead of imitating staff members, patients developed, or refound, their capacity to think about issues and to work for a decision to come to fruition. The community reached the point of a thinking community. It had evolved from a point where thinking belonged to 'the thinkers', and thought was reified (in the form of the concentric circle structure). It eventually reached a thinking function distributed amongst, and belonging to, everyone.

The point of this case study is twofold. The kind of blocks to communication illustrated previously can be refound within the inter-group communication in the community meeting of a therapeutic community. There it is very visible – between patients and staff. Second, we can see how this damages the capacity for the group to take thought and make the best decisions. The latter point is particularly extreme in Phase I. In the staff meeting the characteristic fragmentation of the separate thoughts individuals had was based on an inability to bring differences together fruitfully. The obstacles are – as typically in group dynamics – sustained to ensure more comfortable though unrealistic individual identities.

This chapter has described states of the institution in which its organisation and its thinking can be fragmented. These phenomena derive from the severing of communicational links. These add to a catalogue of boundary phenomena. In answer to the question at the start of this chapter – how do we make the hidden dynamics more transparent? – we now have a number of pointers: blind dramatisations, distorted identities, mutual misperceptions of each other, distorted communication, fragmented thinking. Each of these is an indicator of projective systems in play. Each is a cultural hiatus at the group boundaries.

Whilst this chapter has pinpointed how to spot these deleterious phenomena, which distort individuals and institutional organisation, we are interested in the question: how do we do something about them?

Note

1   Grunberg was a colleague in the establishment of the Marlborough Day Hospital as a therapeutic community in the 1970s and thus a co-worker of mine whose thinking influenced me – and, I believe, vice versa.

CHAPTER 6

Challenge and Paradox

We have seen how the boundaries between disparate groups, sub-groups and cultures are the prime sites to spot institutional pathology. The distortions of communications there will result from highly distorting attitudes held by separate sub-groups. They exist side by side for long periods, even indefinitely, and that creates a damaging rigidity. So, the wish of the 1950s and 1960s to subvert and challenge these institutions was understandable and created a high level of excitement and morale. As I have claimed, that motivation did not necessarily mean the challenges were on the right lines. We must now question those challenges. How much do alternative institutions take into account the deeper level of understanding which we have begun to generate?

The therapeutic community impulse

For those who regard complicity between both sides of the institution, patients as well as staff, as improbable, it is worth recalling how powerful social complicity and coercion is (Asch 1952; Milgram 1969; and see Hinshelwood 1997a). Once *in* the institution, people become signed-up members and hold to the beliefs (however unspoken). And they do so despite the very great problems and disadvantages that beset the institution as a result. The hidden unconscious quality of the force, and often the content, of the belief system makes it very difficult to find a position from which one can adequately see what is occurring. It is truly difficult to penetrate the surface appearances. The problem is to get a fix on what is socially engendered.

Institutions can have a faceless monolithic presence that seems to make the individuals feel insignificant and ignored. Such an experience is well-known, and is exactly that depersonalisation which we have been addressing. If it is the case that complicity in establishing a protective system also creates the viciously inhumane conditions of the institutionalising institution, it is not surprising that there is an equally impressive impulse in the opposite direction. The pressure to conform leads to reactions against – at least it does so on occasions. At various times and places the wish to protest and confront comes intuitively to the fore, as if there is a hidden, but astute, realisation that something is amiss. An impulse towards non-conformity is part of modern history in many spheres; the endeavour to free the inmates of mental health institutions, one of them. It was a liberatory impulse that emerges, or erupts, in a number of forms:

> The impulse is difficult to define. It expresses itself in a number of attitudes: liberalism, egalitarianism, psychological mindedness, toleration of the expression of conflicting ideas, and a kind of shirt sleeves informality about the business of helping people. (Kennard 1999, p.11)

However, as I indicated early on, more is needed than the simple enthusiasm to change things, to free patients who were trapped in mental illness and shackled in mental hospitals. There was then, and there is now, a need to study the specific forms of complicity that are involved.

In the therapeutic community a recognition of this potential, that all members contribute to something that no one individual decides, demands that the dynamics of the institutions as a whole must be a prime focus of attention. This challenge is easier said than done, and particularly it is a hard counsel for patients to have to bear. If the neurotically tormented individual seeks respite from his basic problems through unrelieved attention to his own desires, hopes and distress, he is rapidly jolted if the expectation is to concentrate upon his complicity with others in developing a 'neurotic' institution. On his arrival in a therapeutic community, a suffering individual can be assumed to explore its potential for pursuing his own aims of relief through pooling his efforts with others. He with others can then be thought to press towards specific organisational aims. It is not surprising that considerable resistance might be expected to such a counter-intuitive idea. For both the patient and for the medically trained staff this goes against an ordinary humanitarian response to suffering. Nevertheless this was the birth of the idea of the self-conscious 'therapeutic community'. For the staff, too, many people trained in the ordinary disciplines of care can feel affronted by this reversal of their expectations. It was Bion's undoing at Northfield where he failed to take account of the profound need by patients and staff to individualise suffering within a medical model.

However, for many others this *volte face* in the expectations of their work is a stimulus and creates high morale, a sense of novelty and adventure. Those who feel such a zest for alternative forms often do congregate in therapeutic communities. There can be a heady exhilaration in participating in an institution which is engaged in the subversive activity of dismantling formality.

Alternative task, alternative institution

Since the middle of the twentieth century, reaction to the power and presence of faceless, monolithic institutions grew in Western society as the scope of such institutions steadily increased. Numerous efforts have been made to escape them. Radical and alternative institutions have been experimented with in all sorts of areas of society: public schools, revolutionary communes, kibbutzim, approved schools and prisons, as well as the large mental hospitals (Shenker 1986).[1] Punch (1974) pinpointed 'this desire to escape what is perceived as the deleterious consequences of a permanent social structure in formal organisations as giving rise to the "anti-institution"'. He continued:

> It is an attempt to live perpetually on the margin, resisting the encroachments of formalisation. It is the attempt to retain the spontaneous, immediate, ephemeral joys of 'communitas' against the fate of 'declining' into the norm-governed, institutionalised, abstract nature of law and social structure. (Punch 1974, p.312)

This is no less than the attempt to 'institutionalise freedom', a dream of mankind – and not least in our present age.

Bion's experiment in military psychiatry (page 47) turned into a conflict in which one side 'won' and the other, Bion's, lost. In contrast, Turner (1969) described the relations in alternative institutions as a dialectic, one between structure and *communitas*:

> No society can function adequately without this dialectic. Exaggeration of structure may well lead to pathological manifestations of communitas outside or against 'the law'. Exaggeration of communitas, in certain religious or political movements of the levelling type, may be speedily followed by despotism, over-bureaucratisation, or other modes of structural rigidification. Communitas cannot stand alone if the material and organisational needs of human beings are to be met. (Turner 1969, p.129)

Stanton and Schwartz (1954) used the terms 'formal' and 'informal' organisation to cover 'structure' and *communitas*. We have thus to accept an inevitable tension between authority, structure and formality on the one hand and informal *communitas* on the other. When that tension goes out of balance, we can have something like the extermination camps that Cooper drew to our attention, or of course the rigid large mental hospitals in which personalities were in another way exterminated. Or, alternatively, if there is too much liberalisation, we risk the fate that Punch described. These are the problems of, first, the old-fashioned mental hospitals which crushed the inmates' individuality; and, second, the problem of the reactions against those old institutions, allowing too little formality, structure and authority, as in some therapeutic communities (Baron 1987), with the inherent paradox, 'instituted freedom'. In reacting against the old mental hospital, it is not surprising that the resulting system can at times degenerate into chaos (Foster and Roberts 1998).

Schism

The example of Bion's defeat at Northfield is not about a dialectic of compromise. It was a similar reactive clash between different kinds of authority – medical or military. Different sets of attitudes addressed the same problems, viewed in different ways (medical or military). We therefore have to add the notion that different kinds of authority can destroy each other to the more common notion that authority simply destroys freedoms. This degeneration from a creative tension to a destructive dichotomy is common – and I have described exactly this in the last two chapters, in terms of the individual mechanisms.[2] In focusing on what to do about the institutional pathology, I am about to question, as my first step, how pathologies of the individual and of the institution correspond.

Those split sub-cultures are discontinuous but their discontinuity is interesting. Attitudes abruptly change across a fracture line that exists within the social structure as a 'barrier'. This is sometimes called 'splitting' in the group, or a group 'schism'. Often the kind of paradox that therapeutic communities embody is resolved by such splitting. But the phenomenon of schism in a group produces properties in the social field which do not occur with splitting in the individual. First, splitting in the individual is usually associated with a complete closing down of contact (and communication) between the parts of the person that have been separated by the splitting mechanism (Klein 1946). On the other hand, schism in a group is associated with the adoption of separate and contrasting cultural attitudes over some specific common interest – and mutual communication distortion occurs continuously through projection.

Individuals in an institution often seem to collaborate to express a conflict. This is illustrated in the example of the monologist (page 56), where antipathy within the whole meeting expressed a coherent set of experiences which I have termed a dramatisation. A conflict in the individual becomes an enactment of a conflict in the group, as Ellen engineered (page 55).

In some instances the state of the institution becomes so riven with these expressed conflicts it becomes an enacted fragmentation. It can represent then a very urgent internal state for many of the individuals.[3] Fragmented individuals can effectively collaborate to express their internal state through creating a fragmented organisation. They can collaborate on this effectively by dramatising their failure to collaborate with each other (see Hinshelwood 1987a for a number of illustrations).

The crucial characteristic of working with more severely disturbed individuals is to establish a coherently structured ego, or mind, before that mind can properly have mental problems in it (see Bion 1957). Such individuals create, together, an institution which must continually work to establish a coherent organisation – against the unconscious drive to dramatise disorganisation. Or to put this another way the characteristically disorganised ego of certain individuals is externalised as a disorganised state of the external organisation of the institution. This incoherence in the internal intra-psychic world of the individual leads us to the disarticulated forms of structure or thinking that can be observed in organisations. Thus, the problems of the individual in a mental health system can severely add to the communication problems discovered in institutions. And like the individual, a disordered organisation is severely hampered in its functions, not least in sorting out its own disorder.

Moreover, another serious conflict arises over changing the system. To dismantle those sub-group cultures risks demolishing the specific identities of the individuals constructed by the projective system. And that exposes them to experiences they had been protected from.

Various kinds of paradoxes have emerged in these chapters in Part I: collaborative enacting of isolation; institutionalising informality; democratic hierarchy; and dismantling the unconscious – all pose serious problems for most institutions. For the individual the central dilemma (or paradox) of the human condition in groups is how to belong and to be a person at the same time. This is a core developmental issue in the life of each human being as he enters a social life. The idea of hidden unconscious processes, those that mitigate against the awareness of anxiety, seems to have considerable explanatory value. A number of forms of institutional pathology can be seen to derive directly from the unconscious dynamics: distortions of identity, rigid monolithic institutions, unethical power-relations, communication problems, and schism and fragmentation.

In concluding this chapter here, I interrupt the flow of my argument. To discuss what to do about the pathology of institutions, we need to explore in much more detail the anxiety individuals feel, and its precise expression in collective forms of pathology. To move on to do this I shall devote the next few chapters to this argument.

Notes

1   There is wide variation amongst various therapeutic communities in how much they have dismantled formality, from the Henderson and Cassel Hospitals, with their elaborate structure and organisation (Norton and Hinshelwood 1996), to the Paddington, which abandoned all formality, allowing the patients to organise their own structures (Baron 1987).

2   See Hinshelwood (1996b) for an account of just such a schism within the therapeutic community movement itself.

3   It is a bit like an enactment of the 'world-catastrophe' described by the famous paranoid schizophrenic, Judge Schreber. Freud's 'analysis' of this man suggested that the world around him had, from his point of view, ceased to function as a real world. The psychotic individual in a chaotic organisation has a realisation of that catastrophe.

PART II

Acting and Thinking

Introduction to Part II

In this Part, I propose to develop my view of the individual's anxieties which, ultimately, drive the institutional ones. I will hope to emerge at the end of this Part with some understandable picture of the necessary process of containing those anxieties.

In Part I, I started with institutional phenomena, in particular 'institutionalisation'. In those chapters therefore we looked at the individual from an institutional perspective. In Part II, I shall change the vertex, and begin with the vantage point of the individual in the institution, and then eventually a view of the institution from that individual perspective.

It could be argued that to introduce the individual into social science is a reductionism – it turns social science into individual psychology, and that relegates phenomena at the group/social level to a secondary position, as a less important epiphenomenon. I argue that this is not necessarily the case. What is social is in fact mediated, always, through the actual day-to-day interactions between persons. Though institutional phenomena can be described as such, that reifies them, and the medium in which they form is the complex of individual interactions. The individual cannot be regarded simply as a particle below the level of observation – as a quark might be for a chemist. The individual is the level that carries motivation, anxiety and consciousness, and thus the act of observation itself. The relation of individual to society is therefore more complex than that of component to complete structure.

Much of the work I am reporting comes from therapeutic institutions which have the individual as a prime focus of the task. So, it therefore carries with it a rejection of a simplistic individual-versus-social dichotomy. A more versatile though complex view of the individual–social relatedness is necessary and is implicitly used in clinical practice. So instead, an interactive element between individual and organisation must be retained – there is a mutual interpenetration between individual and social levels.

The actions and reactions of the individual are not restricted to relations to other individuals, but to the whole evolved structure of the collective group of which he is a component member. He has, and experiences, a belonging to the group/society, and embodies in some fashion the group *within* himself. The group/society, as it exists in his perception, is a component of the individual and it belongs to him. The act of awareness in the individual radically changes the conceptual 'emergence/reductionism' gradient, typically of natural science. The individual is born into a group, and retains for the duration of life, a mind populated by a group. The primacy of individual consciousness is based on the fact that it is the only consciousness. But it does not lead to dissolving the existence of a group/institutional-level phenomena, in which the individual is a component, and which is equally a component of the individual.

To a significant extent, the chapters in Part II are an investigation of that manifold complex of super-relatedness between individual and society. Some of this work will depend on small group experience, and despite the specific organisational phenomena and individual experience in small groups, I will take what is common between small groups and large institutions to inform one with the other.

In this Part, we look at the functioning of the individual, with his own conflicts and struggles, to make the best of himself within a troubled institution. In Chapter 7, we will start with some theoretical discussion of the earliest experience an individual has of an institution. There is a fundamental struggle that consumes all individuals – the Oedipus complex as discovered by psychoanalysis. The relation to the parental and family institution from early in life defines important and unconscious aspects of the relation to, and the creation of, institutions in later life. A tripartite typology of identification with, and belonging to, an institution is developed. In Chapter 8, this theory of the primal scene is shown to have deep significance for therapeutic processes in institutional care.

Chapter 9 asserts that not all action is acting-out and that it is important to recognise some kinds of action as healthy and potentially therapeutic in themselves. The key distinction between healthy action and acting-out is the place of reflective thought in the former. This leads in Chapter 10 to a description in detail of interactions in small group therapy and the way individuals and groups may 'contain' each other's emotional states. And this prepares the way for an understanding of the links between individuals in institutional terms.

Chapter 11 develops these conclusions on action and reflection as they apply to the unique feature of therapeutic community practice. That chapter deals with work, work with real responsibility, as a paradigm for therapeutic activities in a therapeutic community. This practice must comprise working with responsibility itself. So, therapy demands close attention to relations that are engaged in during work, and that provide support for, and sharing of, responsibility (rather than as opportunities for the excited and impulsive export of intolerable experience). We can discern the therapeutic advantages inherent in responsible work in the therapeutic community.

CHAPTER 7

The Institution's Primal Scene

In the chapters so far, we have considered the role of the individual and his conflict in the various problems of the hidden community dynamics. I will develop this now, in terms of the individuals' task to come together (and link up) in the institutional structure. Much of this chapter addresses the question: what does the individual bring to his institution? Here, I shall dwell on the central psychoanalytic experience of the Oedipus complex as it is conceived in the young infant. Although this discusses a core feature of human experience, discovered in the individual setting of psychoanalysis, it is the grounding for the later experience of institutions, and I shall continually anchor the concepts in their relevance to the experience of social institutions in later life.

The individual originates in an institution. At the time he first dimly perceives it, he can barely appreciate it realistically. However, the unreality in no way diminishes his emotional reaction to what he cannot properly comprehend. It contributes to a phantastical appreciation of that institution in the family and will extend potentially to phantastical expectations of institutions in general, later in life. We could label these originating experiences the 'early' functioning of the infant (or 'primitive' in that sense of being early in life). Later we shall see how an understanding of these early experiences can help with an important dimension that distinguishes acting-out from a more useful form of action upon which all life must depend.

Primary relations to the institution

The central paradox of the human condition starts very early on in the life of each human being. The core feelings of exclusion (or inclusion) are central for the individual within his social group.

The individual is a group animal at war, both with the group and with those aspects of his personality that constitute his 'groupishness'. (Bion 1961, p.168)

Important experiences derive from this 'war' of the group animal with his groupishness. They might appear totally phantastical, and in a sense they are. The crisis of belonging to a group is that being alone is a danger, whilst belonging requires one to be 'constructed' by the dramatisations of one's group (see Turquet 1975). The claim I make is that however phantastical, they are nevertheless very powerful influences over what a person does when with others. The experience of belonging to, or of *being in*, the community has profound emotional implications and potentially a nightmare quality. I want to explore this in terms of the unconscious phantasies of the Oedipus complex as described by Freud and by Melanie Klein.

The first institution that a person dwells in is the family that comprises two people – the parents – plus a newcomer (the baby/child). In this sense, each individual acquires at the outset of his or her life a paradigm for the institution he belongs to. The model is two people, the parents, together. At some point of development, at some stage in childhood, the two figures of the parents are experienced as together, and with the potential at least to exclude the third party, the child. The claim here is that the sense of an institution is formed and deeply influenced by the early experience of this institution of parenthood, as one's parents actually practise being together. It is up to each of us to decide what to make of such an experience with the dim abilities of the young infant, struggling with its first perceptions.

Freud was particularly concerned in the 'Wolfman' case with what he called the 'primal phantasy' of the parent's sexual intercourse, and how the infant involves himself in it. In that case the patient had not been able to separate himself from the parents; and Freud showed how the patient moulded himself by identifications with alternately the active father or the prone mother. The patient, Freud thought, had become stuck, fixated, in a phase of development in which the infant coped with the sense of exclusion by generating the phantastical idea of *being* one or other of the partners. Thus, being inside the institution (envisioned as parental intercourse) has a number of deeply felt but largely unconscious components.

The inability to separate himself from the parental couple in inter-course, because he is identified completely inside one or the other, leads the child to perceive himself as playing a part, a central part in it. This kind of experience is clearly well removed from actual reality – though to be realistic some children do actually sleep in the parental bed, and many of those can be sexually involved with one or other parent. However, for most of us the experience is a phantasy one, nevertheless its lack of reality is very little restraint on the power that the belief exerts. This of course is very early functioning in the human mind, and the recognition of the unreality of these phantasies is a core struggle in acheiving maturity that lasts in some cases for decades.

Whilst the child or baby manages to feel not separate, he will, in addition, experience the figures of the couple as not properly separate either. They represent some phantastically powerful combination, the so-called 'combined parent figure' (Klein 1932). Often, in phantasy, one resides inside the other. Since, at this stage, phantasies are more powerful than the appreciation of reality, the parents may then be destroyed and in fragments as a result of the infant's aggression aroused by the experience of being excluded. Or, the infant may experience violent and aggressive forms of intrusion into them, and an equal and opposite, intrusive retaliation from them; or finally he may feel his intrusion is met by a hostile and equally phantastical exclusion – the casting out from a promised land.

Experiences of being outside or getting inside the combined parent is shown in the following illustration from a patient of mine in individual psychoanalysis. Aged approximately 40 years, she was still struggling to emerge from the phantasies of this primitive stage of experiencing.

> She repeatedly told me about her journeys on the bus to my consulting room. There was always a great deal of frustration for her and others on the bus, and jostling and minor forms of violence amongst passengers waiting at the bus-stop. Particularly frustrating, enraging and frightening were the moments when the bus arrived and she had to engage in getting onto the bus. She frequently described it to me as 'a jungle out there'. However, there was also an excitement in this frightening scrum at the bus-stop. As we addressed the meaning of this violence in the psychoanalysis, the figures in the phantasy became slightly more distinct. The bus had a driver, and the driver was responsible for driving recklessly so that the passengers in the bus were thrown about dangerously. This, at the level of the infant, is the perception of an intercourse. This dangerous driver in the bus, meant the penis in the vagina, and the patient experienced being *inside* the whole intercourse. However, the particularly crucial frustrations, violence and

fears were attributed to the moments of waiting at the bus-stop and the fight to get on it.

The patient was, in my view, struggling with the phantasy of waiting *outside the couple*, and trying to cope with the violence of her phantasies that were sparked off by the exclusion, the waiting, the competition, and the enormous and violent impulse to intrude right in. Thus separateness, helplessness, and competition were emerging into this patient's experiences (her bus-stop experience). And she could show in her analysis how she continued, in her unconscious phantasies, to get inside the violent intercourse, however terrifying that then was for her.

This illustrates the intensity of experience and feeling that is involved in the position of the 'excluded third'; and the powerful intent to reduce that experience through intrusion into the excluding couple.

Socially shared phantasies

Such primitive relations, more typical of childhood, may be re-experienced continuously in adulthood, in an otherwise apparently real situation. Such hidden phantasies give a meaning – albeit in this case a nightmare meaning – to ordinary life. Quite primitive phantasies of aggression at being excluded from some institution creep into normal reality.

As is well known, Freud thought these experiences are in some measure or other the common inheritance of all persons – the Oedipus complex. The actual details of the phantasies that clothe the experience of exclusion varies between different people, but there is a common denominator. Because they are common to us all they are one way in which people come together as social groups (Freud 1913). Sharing phantasies and beliefs at an unconscious level is a kind of social glue which sticks people together as groups and societies.[1] The earliest forms of these phantasies (Klein 1932), the combination of a maternal figure with a male member that she contains, seem to be established socially as common phantasies, and they are given to us in familiar cultural forms: the 'woman-with-a-penis' or 'castrating woman'. These are ways of talking about figures formed in phantasy but clothed in reality. These figures also attract strong elements of aggression and fear, as well as often a highly exciting quality. Sometimes the nipple is referred to as the penis-in-the-breast, which may then be bitten by the infant, or turned away from in fear. The term 'vagina dentata' expresses an oral version of the violent combination of a female with protruding (male) parts, teeth.

My patient above reacted to the reality of getting on a bus with a driver (the male element inside the female space), with just that fear of aggression.

Very many variants exist of this core unconscious phantasy of the institution of two conjoined figures. Another common variant of this combined parent figure is the socially shared phantasy of a violent husband beating his dependent abused wife. The wife seemingly cannot separate in reality, attempting hopelessly to draw nourishment from the brutally imagined husband/father who has a phallic and cruel dominance. In the case of each of these socially presented figures, the castrating woman and the beating husband, there is a dependent victim, entwined within the combined figure. Thus, the three-person situation, despite much variation, seems to hold at its core a combined male–female structure, suffused with violence together with an inseparable, maybe excited, dependent figure. These are socially endorsed relationships which suggest the persistence of the primitive phantasy of combined parents into stages of the adult personality; that is, these early or primitive phantasies with which the Oedipus complex starts seem to persist in cultural forms into adult life.

In this view, the individual holds a place in a social collective because of the shared experience of these kinds of phantasies. The person, like others, is *in* something that is bigger and stronger than he is. He elaborates these Oedipal phantasies as well as 'finds' them in reality. Elaboration of phantasies into more bland forms helps to master or divert the frustrations, fears and anxieties. To the extent that a person's elaborations are shared they will become included and maybe used for the group's expressive purpose. The elaborations we are concerned with are those that a group or institution can form, and I am referring back to dramatisations, various examples of which we saw in Chapter 4 (see also Hinshelwood 1987a). To the degree that his own phantasy life is somewhat at variance with the majority of the others, he will feel his own inner life imposed upon (or intruded upon) by the group. Such collectively agreed (or imposed) phantasies are an important source it seems of group solidarity; a bed-rock phantasy welds individuals into a place within the group.

Thus, the individuals' early phantasies are deeply embedded in the formation of the later social categories. Because it is a shared common nightmare, each person's willingness to see social institutions in the emotional colouring of this parental structure reinforces the solidarity with each other.[2]

Levels

Clearly these primitive experiences are modified in the process of maturing. The reality, when eventually the infant can perceive it properly, can be a great relief from the nightmare of these Oedipal phantasies. However, a new position with regard to that Oedipal exclusion is not easily attained. It has to be won, with a good deal of 'emotional work'.

The developmental movement forward entails many important changes and developments. Freud's notation is in the form of the child's injunction that he is going to be like Daddy, but not yet, as Freud put it in the Little Hans case (Freud 1909). This kind of identification with the father allows some separateness – it is at first a separation in time, but it implies a separation in space as well – in contrast to the Wolfman, and to my patient in the bus. As the infant begins to feel that the parents love each other, the loving parental relationship is felt to hold things together, the home, the family and the fertile intercourse; and the dominance of love brings out a generally creative outcome to the intercourse – in terms of concern, comfort, enjoyment, nourishment of each other and of fruitful conceptions of babies. This step forward in the process of maturing is described particularly succinctly by Britton (1989):

> The primary family triangle provides the child with two links connecting him separately with each parent and confronts him with the link between them which excludes him. Initially this parental link is conceived in primitive part-object terms and in the modes of his own oral, anal and genital desires, and in terms of his hatred expressed in oral, anal and genital terms. If the link between the parents perceived in love and hate can be tolerated in the child's mind, it provides him with a prototype for an object-relationship of a third kind in which he is a witness and not a participant. A third position then comes into existence from which object-relationships can be observed. Given this we can envisage *being* observed. This provides us with a capacity for seeing ourselves in interaction with others and for entertaining another point of view whilst retaining our own, for reflecting on ourselves whilst being ourselves. (Britton 1989, p.87)

The development of the capacity to know *about* relationships, to be able to witness them from a 'third position', is intimately bound up with the satisfactory development through the early stages of the Oedipus complex, but it also lays down the possibility of developing relations with other institutions – play-group, school, and eventually workplace.

Attaining that witness stance is not gained merely by establishing an emotional link with the parents of love or hate, which are the main emotional dimensions of the Oedipus complex. Instead, the way through the conflict is the possibility of linking through knowing and being known.[3] For instance, news *contained in* the press, which we witness when we open our newspapers, is another experience which has roots in our early relations. We can be sucked into an unknowing, unthinking acceptance of whatever we read as an identification process with the combination – the news *in* the paper. But, in contrast, if we manage to sustain our position as a witness of the process of news contained in the reports, we can begin to think about the news and its reporting in a way that has a quite new dimension.

Literary criticism might be another example, which displays the capacity to take a stance outside the literary contents of emotion, plot etc., and form. The reflective witnessing stance can look at the form and content. Their combination can be observed whilst refraining from a blind involvement with the characters, plot, etc. It is a reserved interest that can acknowledge the love, hate and the rest in it.

This stance allows a flexible movement – a move into the emotions of the primal scene, but a sustained awareness of one's own sense of self and identity. For instance, a member of a theatre audience involves himself in the performing characters that are presented. He does not lose his awareness of the reality but allows himself to be lifted into the performance in which emotionally he participates as if the emotions were his. But, as he is not psychotic, nor grossly disturbed, he has the capacity at the end of the performance to come out of the involved state still relatively intact mentally, and to gather his capacity to think about it if he wants to.

The theatre situation is a relatively voluntary suspension of a separate self, and is a flexible insertion into the witnessed drama. From it one can emerge at will, relatively still the same person, or self. On the other hand, a person in a disturbed state can lose a knowledge of reality, of separateness, and can identify completely with a violent and disturbing couple. Take for example a group of people on a football terrace who become enmeshed in a fight with opposing fans. The involvement becomes less voluntary, to the point even that they can maim and kill each other as if the illusion of football as a war has become a convincing reality of actual war between hostile parties.

Forms of identification

The capacity to learn and think and know from this reflective third position is more truly social. Knowledge exists in contrast to simply *being* in a state of love or hate. When in the social context the capacity to know fades, and over-involvement in these phantasy institutions takes place, it makes the social situation particularly difficult to relate to realistically. A movement to a new level – one of witnessing – and remaining there has important implications for therapeutic institutions. We can ask of any individual in our institutions: where is he or she, in this respect? Does he or she occupy that 'third position' of involved witnessing without unduly intruding or being intruded upon?

The discussion in this chapter has covered several kinds of qualities to relationships. They comprise the following: (a) an *identification*, by equation as it were, with specific figures in an institutional structure – 'being them', without a full appreciation of the distinctness between 'me' and 'them'; (b) an *excluding separation*, grounded in an awareness of that distinction with greater or lesser feelings of exclusion from them – where the intensity of that feeling is greater, there is an agonised pain, which may often be experienced in a paranoid form and gives rise to a fear of hostility between those others, and victimisation by them; and (c) a *third stance*, which is a benign form of the first in which it is possible to experience an 'as if I were them' state whilst holding in reserve a knowledge that one is not in fact them. The last depends also on tolerating the pain of anger, frustration and exclusion in the second.

The centrality of the Oedipus complex in the organisation of the individual personality is a fundamental of psychoanalysis. But here I am taking it up as a fundamental in the experience of an organisation of an institution, too. In answer to the question we opened this chapter with – what does the individual bring to the institution? – we answer that it is the emotional turmoil he found in his very first institution (his family). Developmentally, these experiences precipitate out in the three different forms just summarised, but traces of each will be found inserted in the later life of the individual in greater or lesser proportion, not least in his relation with social institutions. In the next chapter we will look at this in more clinical detail in the developmental processes that make up therapy in institutions.

Notes

1   I would not regard this as the only form of social cohesion, perhaps not even the most significant – we will, in the next chapters, discover others.

2   This is not a pure theory of social construction of identity but a view that bases social construction in the inherent potential for phantasies.

3   Psychoanalysis now distinguishes sharply between emotional relationships (loving and hating), which are part of any authentic relationship on one hand, and the specifically enquiring curiosity that psychoanalysis conducts. Bion, later, referred to these as relationships characterised by 'L' (for loving), 'H' (for hating), and by 'K' (for knowing and being known) (Bion 1962). The last of these is the characteristically therapeutic relationship.

CHAPTER 8

An Institution's Therapeutic Process

In this chapter I want to ask: how do the individual phantasies of the primal scene come to be played out, for good or bad, in the therapeutic institution? And I shall give a clinical illustration of the individual in a therapeutic institution – a day hospital.

We saw in Chapter 5 how a community can come apart as the individuals and the separate groups fail to link in together to create a thinking, communicating community. Here, I shall link similar phenomena to the individual's problem of relating to the primal institution I described in the last chapter. The individual at the centre of the next example appeared initially to lack the ability to think about himself or his environment, the community. In the therapeutic process, we see a resolution of his disturbance and his internal conflicts, which proceeds hand-in-hand with changes in the community towards becoming firmer and more coherent. (This clinical material was originally published in Hinshelwood 1994a, pp.33–35.)

> The Day Hospital had for some time been rather disorganised. The founding Director had left some years before. His staff had slowly drifted away and been replaced. A number of patients remained longer than they should have done. In this Day Hospital, the staff and patients met everyday for a community meeting at 9.30 am. It represented the coming together – the forming every morning. But actually it was ineffective because regularly many would not arrive till after the meeting had finished. An attempt to deal with this attendance problem led to discussion about holding it later in the day. Rather weakly the staff agreed to this. It did not improve matters, the sense of belonging to a coherent community was elusive. Two consequences ensued – the meeting, now held at lunchtime, was only slightly better attended but

afflicted with mutism and apparent sullenness; and in addition the activities of various kinds which had moved to 9.30 to fill in the gap were themselves very badly attended, and this annoyed the staff who tried to run them.

During this time, one of the patients followed an interesting course in his treatment. He was 26 years old, seriously schizoid, though never an inpatient. He took a fairly large overdose of sedatives about 5 days after the changed time of the meeting. He had been one of the poorest attenders, contributed very little and continually complained outside the meetings. He was withdrawn from the community, but had associated with two others, a man and a woman who represented the hard core of the difficulty – poor attenders, unco-operative and seemingly depressed. They complained at most activities and most changes. Overtly these three seemed to have gained nothing from the Day Hospital but their allegiance to each other was important. There was an ambiguity about their relationships, and although the woman changed her allegiance from one to the other occasionally, they remained a tight splinter group. They drew increasing irritation from the staff, and an intimidated respect from other patients who tended to provide excuses for them.

At the meeting on the day when he later took his overdose 'A' had uncharacteristically talked about a memory of his school: he recalled a boy throwing his food on the floor who could not be tolerated by the teachers and had been expelled. 'A' implied the hospital was as unaccepting as the school. This had not been discussed further in the meeting. Instead, discussion had concentrated on the attendance problem, and the illness of the patients that prevented them benefiting from what was offered. In a way 'A' had been expelled from the meeting that day, and in the evening he took his overdose. It was not fatal, but he was away from the hospital for some days, and the community felt a shock at the occurrence.

Though the community was shocked, most of the discussion over the next few days concerned the attendance problem still. The staff had continual, anxious discussion in their own meetings. Eventually they decided to revert to the old time for the meeting – at 9.30 again – and to start a system for recording attendances and dealing with non-attenders (by excluding them for a period).

'A' returned ten days after his overdose, complaining grievously, as always, about the new changes. However, he told the meeting, a couple of days after his return, about a dream he had had the previous night: He was walking along the side of a river. It was phantastically turbulent. He would have fallen in but there was a strong wooden rail which he held on to. One of the other patients pointed out how often 'A' stood at the top of the stairs in the hospital leaning on the rail and gazing down into the stairwell.

This had interrupted the business of that meeting, as on the previous occasion when 'A' had divulged something personal. This time, there was a conflict between not upsetting 'A' who might go and take another overdose, and on the other hand the need to sort out the details of the new arrangements now the meeting was back at 9.30. Thus the meeting appeared to be coming apart in bits with this conflict. A member of staff attempted to bring things together again by using 'A's' dream as a comment on the state of the Day Hospital. He said 'A' was holding on to the Day Hospital because he needed a strong structure to keep him safe – and it seemed that the new arrangements felt strong enough to 'A'. Another patient, X, turned to 'A' and reminded him of the evening he had taken the overdose and they had travelled home on the bus. 'A' had complained that the decision to time the meeting over lunch was out of weakness. 'A' had been very contemptuous and hopeless. X asked 'A' how he felt about the new arrangements for the attendance problem. 'A' sat back in his chair and his face was clouded with thought. Then he sat forward and said, 'Yeah. It's a good idea to try.' It was the first positive, agreeable comment from 'A' for a long time.

Another member of staff summarised his perception of what had happened: On the evening of the overdose, 'A' had a very poor picture of the Day Hospital. It was echoed in many other people's views too. The Day Hospital seemed very weak. Now 'A' (and perhaps others too) seemed to have a picture of the Day Hospital as strong enough to help him. 'A' responded to that quickly at first in his old contemptuous manner, 'What you staff have got in your heads is jelly.' Then he looked around, took a deep breath and seemed to correct himself. 'No. We've got to try the plan they've thought up,' he said decisively. Overnight, when he had dreamed, 'A's' picture of the Day Hospital (his *internal* community) had in fact become stronger for 'A' – not jelly or fragmented. His own decisiveness and positiveness seemed therefore to connect with the solid strength of the *external* community.

Following these events, 'A' became more involved in the Day Hospital as a constructive member; and a change occurred in the trio. It did not split up and the members of it remained friends, but they did seem to disentangle themselves from each other. 'A' found another girl-friend, and the other two became a more exclusive couple together.

This particularly difficult member had responded to the firmer hospital organisation by becoming more able to grasp things decisively in his mind and to hold on to something of the hospital after he left in the evening.

I shall use this example to illustrate important features of the individual's relations to the institution. 'A's' attempt to kill himself seems connected to the weakness of the external organisation of the hospital when it changed the meeting from the early morning. This decision had a self-destructive quality – giving in rather than confronting the real issues. There had been misgivings about it on all sides, not least the staff, who eventually overturned that decision and restored the old timetable and brought about a firm method for handling the attendance problem. Thus, 'A's' relationship with the hospital and its organisation was one in which he inserted himself in a kind of 'identification by equation';[1] he took an overdose when the hospital seemed to be self-destructive.

Later when the community had pulled itself around and became, as in 'A's' dream, strong enough to hold on to, then 'A' could begin to think differently. Some degree of separateness allowed him the capacity to witness the community so that he could think *about* it. Thus 'A' who had hitherto taken evasive action against the experience of being the 'excluded third' could move towards taking up the 'third position', the witnessing stance (see page 84). In the process, he developed a more positive relationship with the institution, the day hospital.

The separateness, in my view, was connected with the staff's capacity to work together (their thinking 'intercourse') over the problem. Some could keep in mind a picture of a firm organisation, even when it seemed to be disappearing from the external organisation. The staff holding this internal community together are in a position to enable the patients also to hold something together inside themselves as well.

In the mind of a patient, there is a specific relationship with a container, something that is robust and supportive (see Hinshelwood and Skogstad 1998, as well as the illustration on page 94 in this book, from Santos and Hinshelwood 1998). The container in the social group is represented by the institution, therapeutic community or the hospital staff. This containing relationship[2] in a therapeutic form promotes the internalisation of the community organisation as a potential support and container into the intra-psychic organisation of the individual personality. But there are abnormalities of that relationship. One is the aggression towards the assisting external structure which disturbs the process of internalisation so no whole or functioning understanding can be felt inside the person – as for 'A' initially in the example. We will come back to the role thinking plays in preventing 'identification by equation' when it intervenes between impulse and action in Chapter 9, where I will develop the notion of a containing institutional structure in which active work is done.

Notes

1   See page 86. I use this term with an awareness of the allusion to 'symbolic equation' (Segal 1957) which I intend. I shall not pursue this connection but it is part of the spectrum of omnipotent forms of relating (see Hinshelwood 1993b).

2   I do not propose to go into details about the psychoanalytic view of 'containment'; but see Gomez (1997) or 'Containment' in Hinshelwood (1989a).

CHAPTER 9

Abuse and Acting-Out

The mental hospital institution has to contain the anxiety imported from society. It does so in ways that are more or less useful; and these we can say are the relations of containing. Containing can be understood in terms of the relation a baby makes when crying in distress. And mother thereby alarmed must reflect on the baby's need. The containing substance is the mind of the other, the mind of mother for the baby, or the mind of others in the social context. In fact, in the course of development for the baby, his mind has to come to contain his own experiences, and to understand himself. Infants mindlessly scream, but, at times, the violence with which an adult, too, may express himself seems uncontained and mindless. Certain adults require a special structure. But often it is so great a violence as to stretch the containing function to its limits. There is now a developed psychoanalytic theory of 'containment'; it describes an intimate relation between the individual's own internal difficulties and the external conditions of the organisation to which he is always related. The patient in psychiatric care can come to a degree of better containment of his own experiences, and thus to enhance his mind with a little greater capacity to understand those experiences which drive him mad. In the example in the last chapter, 'A's' ability to think independently about his community and himself increased.

I shall describe a brief illustration in which the patient used the structure in a very different and extreme way, both the structure of the community, and also the particular couple, composed of her key nurse and her therapist. Maria (a patient of Angel Santos, described in Santos and Hinshelwood 1998, pp.31–34), an adolescent admitted to the Cassel Hospital, had been sexually abused from an early age by some of the frequent visitors to her young single mother. She has used several psychotropic drugs, sometimes with her mother and sometimes on her own. She had sniffed gas, and used to cut herself deeply in the forearms. Most of the time she was 'out of her mind'.

During her assessment, she spoke of 'Two Marias', one excited and dangerous (the one who took drugs and cut herself), and the other wanting to keep herself safe and face change. Some months after admission, her self harming and suicidal behaviour escalated to the extent that a 24 hour observation rota by staff and patients had to be organised to keep her safe.

This pattern was highlighted during the assessment process. In her life previously, she would create situations in which she had to be physically restrained in order to keep her safe. She was known to the security staff of her local shopping centre where she used to create disturbances by doing such things as breaking windows. On numerous occasions she had to be physically held so that she would not do more damage.

She recreated this dynamic within the community, and at different levels. At times during her individual psychotherapy she would start by saying she felt she could just jump from the window of the office. In the countertransference the therapist felt she needed to be 'held' psychologically or her psychic world would fragment into the psychotic state into which she had occasionally fallen in the past.

This conflict was eventually enacted at the level of the community during a week in which her cutting and overdosing increased. She engaged staff and other patients in keeping her safe. She let them know that she had injured herself and then rushed out of the hospital with patients and staff having to bring her back into the hospital and stay with her on a 24 hour basis.

The enquiry into the dynamics of her relationship with the community demonstrated how she had orchestrated a particular dramatisation of an internal conflict. It appeared she had projected the part of herself who kept her alive into the community. She, in turn, played the excited, suicidal role. The internal conflict over whether she should live or die had been externalised.

The internal conflict inside Maria, between a despairing and deadly intention, and a part of herself that wants to live, became visible in the structure of the community around her. People were not just performing their professional roles (as staff or patient); they also played out a role in Maria's internal conflict. At the time when Maria was most disturbed and her acting out escalated to a dangerous degree of self-harming behaviour, the different attitudes, experiences and feelings of her nurse and her therapist, as they each worked with Maria, were explored. The relationship between nurse and therapist became clear during a supervision session in which both the workers met with a senior member of the clinical staff.

On one hand, Maria's nurse was despairing about the situation and the future possibilities of treatment. She felt that Maria's destructive behaviour was irreparable and that she should be transferred to another hospital suited to containing acute psychiatric disturbances. The therapist who had not been directly involved in having to restrain Maria was more hopeful on the other hand about the potential for change. He felt that we should continue trying to help and treat Maria here.

The nurse felt angry and unsupported, feeling that Maria had succeeded in 'seducing' the therapist into not realising the dangerousness of her behaviour. The therapist felt disappointed that the nurse was not trying hard enough and that if only Maria could be contained longer she would be able to use the therapy for change. It was proving difficult to reach any happy compromise or synthesis of the two positions.

It also became apparent that the split between the two workers had a strong resonance with the split in Maria's internal world, in which there was one hopeful 'Maria', who wanted to face change, and a despairing 'Maria', who wanted to give up, destroy the treatment and to kill herself. This understanding pointed towards the forces keeping the two sides apart and to how this split was being repeated in the nurse–therapist relationship.

As Maria flung herself towards death, as she rushed out of the hospital, the community was impelled equally impulsively to rush to pull her back. Thus, actions by the community, too, which might look like therapeutic work, could also be termed 'acting-out', where there is a sense in which a patient's internal state (in this instance, a conflict over living or dying) is exported into another person, or into a structured group of others. They react in non-reflective ways, often helpless and inseperable from the patient's own impulses.

Surviving or discharging abuse

This is an extreme example of that intrusive identification I termed 'identification by equation'. At the end of Chapter 7, we summarised three kinds of identification: (a) a form of identification in which there was an *equation* of the person with the object identified with; (b) an identification as the excluded one, left out of the object, in which envy, hatred and violence permeate; and (c) a more empathic identification involving knowing that one is separate from some other institution. The first of these is important as it abolishes thought or the capacity to experience the real situation, upon which any containing of oneself might depend. It excludes reflection and it short-circuits straight from the experience to discharge. It is possible to look at this in formal terms, using the paradigm that Jaques [1953] (1955) spelled out:

> Individuals may put their internal conflicts into persons in the external world, unconsciously follow the course of the conflict by means of projective identification, and re-internalise the course and outcome of the externally perceived conflict by means of introjective identification. (Jaques [1953]1955, p.497)

We have been making a distinction: on the one hand, an explosive event that seems to discharge the whole situation from someone's mind, and dissipates it in the institution; or, on the other, a more potentially thoughtful reflection on the event in which the person can 'follow the course of the conflict' in Jaques' terms. In therapeutic situations that reflective activity is usually performed at first by the minds of the staff. The issue is whether the minds of patients, too, can come to do it in a reflective way – or can they only use their minds to discharge it into the external structure.

In the example of the day hospital (Chapter 8), 'A' moved from 'identification by equation' to the witnessing stance. However, Maria remained in the first kind of identification with her institution, exporting herself straight into the structure of the hospital, and into the experiences, minds and relations of the others in the social institution, where independence of thought and action have become impossible.

Such explosive acting-out is often the resort of people who have suffered abuse in reality. They fear the violent intrusion of abuse but are impelled to visit it upon others – especially their helpers. We have to contain the vulnerability and the disruption of interiority itself. The intrusive form of identification has the quality of a violation. Maria was an example of the explosive intrusiveness which is the trademark of certain kinds of survivors of abuse – those that survive very poorly, in fact.

The term 'acting-out' is apt as aspects of identity are, in a peculiarly literal sense, exported *out* into another's identity. In the process, separate identities are no longer sustained, but become confused with each other. Maria's 'use' of the staff – and also of other community members in her projection of her internal conflict – relieves her of her internal stress. This is not 'internal work' in the constructive sense, yet it is work upon the internal state. The projecting out is an acting-out.

Such people are those who are more than society can cope with – and who our institutions have to contain. Very many people who require institutional forms of treatment have been the victims of abuse that has disastrously violated their private boundaries (Norton and Hinshelwood 1996). Frequently, therefore, their mode of relating involves violent behaviour or severe self-harming which destroys the necessary boundaries of a helping institution. But even if they use words and ordinary communications, invariably they have a quite extreme impact. Instead of ordinary communication, a kind of acting upon the minds of others takes place – a kind of 'psychic' action, as it were, which violently effects the receiver of these actions. This is what we have to contain in our institutions.

On the whole, they either have problems of engaging and sustaining relationships, including therapy relations or they have profound difficulties in sustaining meaning in relationships, and to acknowledge the purpose of symbols for containing meaning. It is not that they don't have relationships; they use relationships with others in quite unusual ways – invariably to encroach upon others psychologically, so that they endanger the balance of mind of both. That person and those intruded upon then tend to relate and to act without reflection, on impulse instead, as if, in a real sense, the boundaries of interiority for both are ruptured. Identities have been confused.

Bion (1962) and Segal (1975) have both dwelt on the significance of the communicative form of projection, and this is important in working in a formal psychoanalysis towards raising the issues from non-verbal to verbal communication, and from unconscious to conscious awareness. When it comes to the severely disturbed patients like Maria, we cannot rely on that necessary hope which underpins the patient's communications. Instead, the staff group is subjected to use by the patient for other desperate but more destructive aims. Maria, for instance, after her discharge from the hospital, did badly and eventually ended up in prison where she was diagnosed as schizophrenic and removed to a secure psychiatric unit.

I am stressing the important distinction between the exported kind of identity by equation (involved in acting-out) and on the other hand the capacity to think about those feelings in a reflective manner, which can give them a new meaning, perhaps more constructive, and is also communicable symbolically. So, acting-out causes problems for the therapist accustomed to using words for communication. This distinction forms a specific dimension on which are stretched out the forms of relating. At the non-separation end of the dimension, a relationship occurs in which a communication has an impact as if it were a violent intrusion upon identity. Whereas at the opposite end projective processes effect communication of feelings, which in the right circumstances can be reflected upon.

This connects with the inter-group communication problems, described in Chapter 5. There we viewed them from the perspective of the institution. Here, we have encountered them from the perspective of the individual, albeit in quite extreme form.

Action and reflection

In the restricted encounter in a psychoanalytic setting, all actions are acting-out, whether they are psychic or physical action. But, action is a necessary part of life. In a social context, it cannot be dismissed as it has to be in a psychoanalytic setting. The discussion above, coming from an active practice like the therapeutic community, shows up the kinds of actions which involve thoughtless discharge from the mind, and in contrast thoughtful action that involves reflection.

The distinction between communicating and acting-out, as it has become in psychoanalysis, is a spurious distinction. Instead acting-out ought to be contrasted with healthy action, not with communication. There are thus two kinds of action: one is A + T, action based on thought; and A − T, thoughtless action, or acting-out, with a completely different aim, that of discharging experience. Communication is not simply the verbal transmission of information, as it might at times be considered in a psychoanalysis. Communication can involve the direct impact of one mind on another (see Heimann 1952). When action of the acting-out kind occurs, there is a loss of the capacity to think, to have regard for the consequences of the action, or to consider the objects into whom projections are made. The patient intrudes so much into the identity of others (e.g. the staff) that both patient and staff proceed and act as if there is a concrete equation of the patient (or part of the patient) with the other person.

In the case of Maria, just given, staff, like the patients, get caught up unthinkingly in roles which patients have unconsciously assigned them to play. They are roles that replicate aspects of the patients themselves. They are in effect dramatisations, not in the 'safety' of a group therapy, but in the hurly burly and risk of everyday life. In healthy action, reflection intervenes between experiences and ensuing action. Insofar as reflection occurs, and is embedded as it were, in the subsequent action, the action will inevitably express the thought in some form (see the example of Cath later in Chapter 13). There is potentially a communicative aspect of ordinary action. Consequently, actions can be used better, at times, and in ways, and with people, where verbal interpretation might well be lost. In institutions much of the proper interaction is actually at the level of action of one mind on another. There is a contrast between the thinking, reflective and verbal mode of a psychotherapy and the *active* mode of an institution.

For people with certain kinds of difficulty, a therapy based on activities may be a treatment of choice – instead of, or prior to, a verbal therapy (we will consider more practical aspects of such treatments later, in Chapter 11). These are the people where reflection is squeezed out and action is impulsive acting-out. They tend to have severe personality disorders, act impulsively and explosively upon others' minds, as Maria did; or psychotic patients who destroy their minds for thinking, on a long-term basis. Those categories of disorder are precisely the ones which therapeutic communities have become adapted to contain and treat.

Those members of staff, and others, caught up in this way have to develop special means for supporting the capacity for reflection on what is happening to them. The capacity to reflect, and to insert reflection between experience and action, has come to the fore again. It had also emerged from the problem of tolerating the Oedipus phantasies (Chapter 7). And we previously met the problem of reflection in the example of the community that could not think (Chapter 5). I shall move on to the further vicissitudes of reflection in the next chapter.

CHAPTER 10

The Group as a Containing
Reflective Space

Institutions engaging with patients who short-circuit their own thinking and reflecting on their experiences need to establish specific means for developing the capacity to reflect, as a function of the institution. In this chapter we will consider the question: how might the capacity for reflection be enhanced? It is useful to think of the institution itself as having a 'reflective space'. To look more closely at this interaction between the organisational structure and the internal coherence of the individuals, I propose to turn for a moment to small group therapy. Groups may develop a culture in which the individuals' emotions are adequately and sympathetically responded to. There is a space, as it were, in the group where emotion can be tolerated and reflected on if necessary. However, in addition, that reflective space inside groups can tear itself apart. The culture may develop to block empathetic links with others as if the group and the individuals are closed to each other.

What I will focus on is the quality of linking; specifically the linking between persons in a group, but this has an intimate connection with the linking that goes on within the minds of the individual person in that group or organisation. In Chapter 4, we focused on the way in which individuals become involved (identified) with their group or community through specific roles in unconscious dramatisations. Grunberg (Chapter 5) described the development through concentric circles as a phase of clarification before a more realistic thinking could take place. Clearing the inner ring in the formation of a community after-group created a space in the centre of the large group, that dramatised an internal space in which the community personality could be reflected on and understood. So, originally a culture which resembled psychotic thinking at the community level moved slowly to a structure that allowed thought to develop. Thought as linking together separate points of view in some lively relationship replaced it, and was dramatised as the integration of separated groups and individuals.

Authentic thinking is not to be conceived simply as the property of an individual; it also depends on the context. It needs a structure which supports the capacities for reflection of all who are present. To develop a mentality consistent with mature thought depends on the state of the group, its atmosphere or culture, as well as the individual person. During a group session, one can ask at any point in time: what sort of link is a person seeking? And what sort of link is offered by 'the group' in response? I use the term 'link' to mean the activity in a group; the link is the action of one mind on another. A thinking mind brings together two thoughts with a link between them; we say, 'putting two and two together'; whilst there is also an important external linking. Two people come together in specific links, notably sexual coupling, but as importantly, there is a mental, emotional linking, not just agreeing with each other, but understanding each other's emotional states, 'where they are coming from', we say.

In Chapter 7 we discussed one of the most potent sources of violence and aggression in institutions, the Oedipal sense of exclusion. This is a paradigm of the problems that linking entails. A link is not an easy matter, it may involve that turmoil of potential, anticipated or real exclusion from the object linked to.

I suggested that exclusion is a powerful activating force in organisations. When one group meets another, each member of one group is perforce excluded from the other group, and *as a group* the members are confronted with the experience of exclusion. And this can lead socially and politically to inter-group violence from which a vast proportion of the history of human civilisation has been made. Within a group, though, members may fluctuate between the two levels of involvement – the primitive form of identification by equation or the capacity to be an involved reflective witness who can reflect as a separate person on the group relations. This kind of fluctuation is of great importance in gauging the therapeutic process in small group therapy.

I shall now examine the fate of this reflective process in small groups. Smaller and more circumscribed than a therapeutic community, a therapy group gives easier access for observation. In such groups, people link together by reflecting each other through their reactions, rather like a mirror. People take in personal communications from each other and reflect, in emotional and cognitive ways, on them. Thus, people link together emotionally, intuitively and unconsciously. At other times, individuals are left very much on their own with their emotional states. Then, despite sitting together in the same room, and despite being physically adjacent and engaging at times in verbal exchange, they remain emotionally isolated; no others seem to engage or become involved or reflectively contain each other.

I will give brief illustrations of these states in a therapy group. In the first session, the 'space' allows adequate linking to occur:

> Two men in a group were discussing a trivial detail about some maintenance work on a car that belonged to one of them. 'A' described his difficulty with a rusty bolt. 'B' talked about how he had once had the same problem and had solved it by hitting the bolt with a hammer; he seemed pleased with himself. Another man, 'C', gave a slight laugh and remarked on 'B's' hint of pride. 'A' looked startled and then a little angry, as he realised that he had given 'B' the opportunity to be pleased with himself. He told 'B' that it was no solution to hit the bolt with the hammer and explained why. Clearly he now wanted to put 'B' down. Two women in the group were looking on with some fascination at this male sparring. One said 'Men!' with mock exasperation. The other said her husband had returned from a football match recently with a bruise on his cheek which he had refused to talk about.

In this interchange five people were involved who seemed willing to tune in, in their own characteristic ways, to the male rivalry and psychological bruising which was going on. People seemed to respond consciously and unconsciously to the emotional colour that another person expressed. These things were intuited and responded to – partially in the conscious verbal content and partly at an emotional intuitive level. The talk was not necessarily harmonious, respectful or friendly. But they were reading each other accurately. It is that quality of being 'in tune' which I am emphasising.

Verbal interaction is a carrier of emotional contact; but in the next group session it is as if there is no proper recognition of each other's emotional states. They do not take in, as a communication, the emotions put out by others. The following material shows a 'cutting off' process which results in a bleak atmosphere in the group.

> In another group a woman, 'X', described an event in which her husband had had a row with her mother. Another woman, 'Y', waited just until this story had finished, and immediately asked for the dates of a forthcoming break in the group sessions. They had been announced recently. The therapist pointed out how 'Y' had cut across the first woman's story. She had also cut out her own memory of the dates. 'Y'

immediately turned to enquire of someone else. A man started to talk about his mother-in-law, seemingly following the first woman, though clearly absorbed only in his own tale – more to do with seeking out a mother for himself because in childhood he had spent long periods separated from his own mother.

In this group there is a considerable cutting across each other's communication, or using another's communication in order to divert to one's own without linking into the other person's state of mind. The verbal content of each contribution makes an almost calculated disconnection from the emotional tone of the previous speaker. There is plenty of talk, but no linking. A contribution from one member severs the links that could have been made with the contribution of the preceding speaker. We see a sort of attack upon emotional linking, and a culture in the group that militates against knowing each other. The lack of linking then leaves each of the members isolated; and the group culture is coloured by a frustrating irritation, so that the group is dominated by a repetitive replaying of old stereotyped roles and subjects. In this sense, there is a severe restriction of the mental space for reflection within the group. The space to reflect has shrunk.

Various links

The members are inhibited and repressed, and their verbal communications almost completely fail to carry emotional impact. It differs in appearance from that explosive enactment in the last chapter (page 94); and is a more common occurrence than the impulsive physical action that occurs typically in living-together communities. However, both kinds of activity abolish reflection. We could say that the shared phantasy is to shun any institution and linking that might be witnessed. In this case the institution that is shunned is the group – and by shunning the institution of the group, they abolish any coherent institution from which to feel excluded. Of course this results in a bleak experience of involvement in nothing. However, in the next example, there is an occurrence of an explosion, related to what we saw with Maria (page 94). At least then there is something to get excited or shocked about. Sometimes, an individual will thrust into the group a very high charge of emotion, so intense that other members of the group will be unable to respond. Then various things happen: the group may freeze in silence (as in the illustration below) or they may distract into other activity, or retaliate with powerful projections in return.

When a person puts into the group a powerful emotional moment we can envisage the reflective space as operating as a container. It may successfully accommodate the emotion, or conversely the container may lack that capacity to accommodate emotions and the impact dismantles the reflective space, sometimes explosively. Then the reflective space will close off, or split up and go to pieces or will become retaliatory. The following brief example is a group which is asked to contain an emotional impact, first of sexual shock, and then of aggression delivered as if bullets from a gun. (Some of this material was first published in Hinshelwood 1994b.)

> A rather stiff woman, 'R', spoke briefly and emotionally about certain sexual practices her husband demanded of her, and which troubled her. She appeared unemotional when divulging this. An embarrassed silence fell on the rest of the group. The therapist pointed out how the feeling was redistributed – the woman's feeling disappeared and the others felt her embarrassment. Then a man, 'S', started talking in a moral way about perversions in general and about the wicked ways of the world, and his own mournful misfortunes. His insensitivity to others and to their embarrassment provoked annoyance. Another man, 'T', said that 'S' was dominating the group. A quarrel began. 'T' became more and more loquacious with his list of complaints about 'S', the insensitive man. As this excited anger increased, 'S' shrank into a hurt protest under the accusations. 'T', the angry accuser, suddenly jumped up out of his seat and stood over 'S', pointing his finger and jabbing at 'S' as if firing each accusation like a bullet from a gun. When he stopped his accusations, 'T' was quite still for a moment. Then as if deeply embarrassed he abruptly left the room. Several innocuous comments were made before the end of the group.

There is a high level of emotional tension, anxiety and anger in this session. It circulates without ever properly being linked into by other members: first the embarrassed silence, then 'S's' self-involved monologue, and finally 'T's' dramatic outburst. This group did not have the capacity of a reflective space, to contain these individuals' experiences. The whole containing vessel, the reflective space, depends on the quality of the emotional linking – in this example the link is like that of a bullet in wounded flesh – which destroys the container it seeks.

Types of containers

In these illustrations we can see varying kinds of containing with varying degrees of success. I shall point to three general types.[1]

First, the contents are so vibrant and explosive that the whole container is exploded and disabled with an uncontained result. In the last example, the group *exploded* as 'T' fired his emotional bullets, and then literally left the group.

Second, the container is so rigid that it does not allow any real expression of the contents which are then simply moulded to the containing space; the group froze in an embarrassed silence when 'R' had spoken of her sexual relationship with her husband – the group itself became frigid, a frozen rigidity.

Third, both the container and the contents adapt and mould in response to each other, so that both are able to develop and 'grow'. In the first example on page 102, people did *link* to each other with a depth of emotional understanding, albeit about male rivalry.

In a therapeutic group, we examine the relation between the individual with his overwhelming experiences which he cannot make sense of, and the group of others into which he expresses those experiences. The group may explode and fragment, or it may crush the individual and his experience into meaninglessness. Or, there may be some negotiated arrangement for both to co-exist through understanding, adjustment and development. We are interested, as therapists, in this third possibility, the flexible containing of group and individual which offers a possible therapeutic influence.

The disorganisation of the group's linking – emotional, cognitive and interpersonal – is the equivalent of the psychotic dismemberment of an individual's mind. The group state is an enlarged version of the psychotic attacks on mental linking. In a group, even a neurotic person can make attacks on linking (Hinshelwood 2001). The task of a group therapist is to oversee the reflective space in which links are made or attacked. He is not a neutral bystander. His own mind represents the trigger for prompting the reflective space into action when necessary. It is not necessarily easy, since the therapist is a member immersed in the same culture that affects all.

In the longer example to follow, I give a sample of a therapist's struggle to use his own mental space to generate a reflective space in the group.

'J' was describing a familiar situation in which he sat alone at work in the coffee break, wrapped in his miserable sense of loneliness. Briefly he paused for breath and a woman, 'K', brightly remarked on her own work and the various attractive features of her boss for whom she was an efficient personal assistant. He had taken the trouble to make her a cup of coffee when she was typing some urgent letters for him. This was a little provocative for 'J', and for the group, as she was normally critical and scathing about her boss whom she regarded as rather useless. 'L', a supercilious man, was amused and ironic about her change of view. Before 'J' could resume his complaints about his own lack of friendship, 'M' intervened with his usual irritation. He pointed out how 'L' trivialised 'K's' communication. 'L' reacted in mock startled fashion as if he was bewildered by such a construction of his comment. 'J' eventually intruded in characteristic fashion, starting with a quite insightful view of 'K's' overt sexual slaving for her boss. Then, he described one of the secretaries at work – 'J' often told us that the secretaries were sexually tantalising for him – who had refused to do anything for him when he had an urgent report to do. This led on to more moroseness about his own lack of success with the secretaries – either sexually or in the work.

At this point, I intervened because I felt the patterns of communication invited, in fact put pressure on, me to do something about the way 'J' dominated, and left so little chance for interaction and communication between the other members. I was familiar with the pressure on me to rescue the group from 'J', and in the past I had made many attempts to help the group to see something of 'J's' masochistic posturing, and his overt excitement at getting everybody else in a state of exasperation with him. Such remarks of mine had tended only to raise the frustration towards 'J' as his behaviour was made clearer and more obvious to them. In contrast, 'J' invariably responded as if my remarks had gone straight through him and out again without leaving any trace. I did not want to continue this kind of interpreting which left me as frustrated as the rest of the group, and to no apparent avail.

On this occasion I reflected on my impressions in this and in recent meetings of the group. I realised it was not just 'J's' method of communication but many of the communications from others could also be equally unconnected. In particular, in this sequence:

1. 'K' made a comment about her boss to distract from 'J' and as a way of boasting unkindly about her working relations, thus dissociating herself from him.

2. 'L' side-stepped 'K's' 'success' with her boss and instead he referred to her contradiction about her boss (in reality 'L's' own pre-occupation with satisfactory sexual coupling).

3. Then 'M' pointed out how 'L' had devalued 'K's' communication, as if he protested, but thus blocked any recognition of 'L's' hidden fears.

4. 'L' then overtly dismissed 'M's' irritable comment with his mild mocking.

5. 'J' diverted from his own insightful link with 'K's' covert sexual flaunting, and returned to his maudlin pre-occupations.

I also noticed the withdrawal and isolation of a couple of other members who were silent throughout this sequence. One was a woman who is working through the possibilities of a divorce from a husband with whom there is no adequate communication, overt or emotional.

Having taken thought in this way, I then told the group my reflections and demonstrated the way in which each of the communications, though conveying some content on the surface, was *doing* something else; that is, they were leaving the last person's comments hanging unheard in some essential and emotional way. On each occasion when someone spoke, a potential emotional link was brought to a halt. In short, each participant was abandoned in turn, left alone in the group and divorced from the companionship of others.

My intervention along these lines may well have been less systematic and less clear than the presentation here, but I experienced a significant change in the atmosphere of the group after I had finished speaking. My attention was particularly drawn to 'J' who was looking directly at me by the time I had finished. The eye contact between us was most unusual for him since he typically looked at the floor throughout the sessions. 'J' said, 'You mean that the others are as bad as me?' It was clearly an arresting thought. There had been not just eye contact, but a contact at a much deeper level of 'J's' thinking – at least for that moment.

This illustration conveys how the therapist's thoughtful reflections, when conveyed to the group, did successfully change the quality of communication. Initially linking was actively thwarted, but towards the end of the illustration the group was a potential mental space, in which the individuals were linked by their emotional experiences impacting on one another. In general, a group functions therapeutically in so far as it manages to create a culture of emotional linking between individuals so that it becomes a container in which the members' experiences can be accepted and responded to. This gives them a form *within the group* and can then be reflected upon by the group and the individuals concerned. The movement towards reflection was based, at an individual level, in the general attainment of that third witnessing position, the observing stance. And it is a movement within individuals that is co-ordinated as a shared movement with others.

This prompts the question of how to establish this shared movement which enhances the mental life of the individual – or perhaps it is better phrased as: how to prevent the opposite movement, away from that openness to contact and reflection. The rest of this chapter will briefly address certain possible solutions.

Cultural containers

The cultural container is a mutual responding between individual and group. The individuals both set up a characteristic kind of linking (and thus a type of containing culture), and they are also affected by that linking with a response that further determines the continuance of a linking culture.

At the larger level of the institution, we can recall, in Chapter 5 (page 65), the community was in a structural state in which group activities were severed from each other. Communication was visibly absent, as displayed in the community meeting. In that example a structural approach was employed in order to get the separate and isolated groups into greater communication with each other. I suggest that what we see in a small group setting amplifies our understanding of the community problem. Whereas a structural approach may be the appropriate method at the community level, it is clear the emotional relations are what is under attack. If we think back to the examples of communication distortion, in Chapter 5, it is the perception of another group, *in emotional terms*, that is the potent force in the distortion of communication (the example on page 63). Some 'other' group is seen in extremely *bad* terms and effective communication is lost. The culture of a community, like a small group, can therefore be expressed in terms of its quality of emotional linking. Or to put it another way, the crucial cultural components for therapeutic purposes are the emotional links and the degree to which they succumb to attack. Emotional linking between different sub-groups is important at the organisational level, bearing in mind that the emotional state of a sub-group is the common emotional state of the individuals – the emotional common denominator of those holding a place within the group.

Intrusions upon the reflective space

If a mental space exists within an individual where mental contents enter into relationships with each other to form thoughts, coherent arguments, sequences of feelings, narrative phantasies etc., we also know that this psychic space in the individual can have other properties. Mental contents may be pulled apart, made separate, isolated or split up in the person's mind. Bion (1959) described that splitting up as 'attacks on linking'. It is the core problem of the psychotic – he pulls apart his own mind, cannot perceive reality, and he fragments his thinking.

Therapeutic institutions, like individual minds, and like small group therapy, also have reflective problems. They may be beset by intrusions into their reflective space when individuals cannot contain their own experiences and seek 'identity by equation'. And being disturbed by institutions, the violence against institutions, abolishes any relation to it. A specific institutional phenomenon of this kind was pointed out by Main (1967), who noted that so often organisations become unthinking and monolithic. Though they develop innovatory projects, something so often takes over which, in the course of time, renders that service stale, institutionalised and seemingly lacking in humanity (Griffiths and Hinshelwood 2001). Main was not content to say it was merely the product of time. Instead, he described how time sees the generation of characteristic dynamics. Good ideas and theories become mental objects inside the minds of the staff (and patients of course), but are gradually subject to a curious distortion.

Working procedures in organisations are normally the result of problem-solving arising from a flexible approach to real problems. They are reality-based solutions, which are then handed on from one generation to another. But, in this intergenerational passage, they change to become 'the way things are done' – they ossify and become rigid and unthinking. Memories of why they are done this way are forgotten, often quickly, and a moral tone, '*We* do it this way', takes over from the original practical one. Main talks of this distortion as a 'hierarchical promotion'; the idea changes its residence from the ego to the super-ego, remembering gives way to moralising. Starting in the thinking parts of the ego, as solutions to particular problems, they later move into a fixed morality and achieve a super-ego quality: this is how things ought to be done, because the older generation did it so. In community terms it stops being a realistic solution and becomes an unthinking ritual. Useful practices, now moral beliefs, hinder further creative thought and new solutions. The institution's practice declines into ritual unthinking performance, and reflection ceases.

To conduct one's practice on the basis of received wisdom saves the individuals from the emotional uncertainty and anxiety that would come from new thinking about *current* problems now. Under the pressures of anxiety, people are freed from thinking, and become eventually possessed by the institution's practice. The individuals experience the received wisdom as a kind of institutional super-ego and feel dominated by it. They are required to internalise these practices as they enter the institution, and they may experience them as 'enforced introjection', as Menzies (1959 [1990], p.460) said. The result is a powerful object inserted inside the individual. This super-ego-like object is an institutional intrusion into the private interior.[2] It demands a kind of blind acceptance which feels persecutory, and, like the abusive intrusions of many of the patients, it achieves a restriction of the capacity for thought (Berlin 1958; Kennedy 1993; Segal 1977).

An institution or community that has given up fresh problem-solving in favour of ritual performance can become cut off in many ways from what is happening around it – that is to say, it fails to react to changes in demand from its funding organisation, in the pattern of its referrals, in the climate of opinion about communities or therapy (the Magic Mountain syndrome – van den Langenberg and de Nastris 1985). In addition it becomes ossified in its routines, a lack of vigour and an allegiance to procedures for their own sake take over from a full community life. It becomes a pale version of itself. Its own demise often comes swiftly, but always unexpectedly.

The culture of enquiry

These time-honoured practices, no longer reflected upon and not linked with actual persons or issues any more, are difficult to change. Main advised counteracting this 'freedom from thought' with what he called a 'culture of enquiry', as part of the institution itself. A culture consciously aimed at questioning and reflecting on why we do things like this is needed, and in a therapeutic community is instituted (Norton 1992). To sustain a process of thinking about 'the way things are done', we must continually ask, 'What is the problem that this is a solution to?'; then we might recharge a respect for reality. But, questions seem to defy that moral authority of tradition; and a fight has to go on to keep open a space in the working day, but more importantly a space within the minds of the professionals, a space where questioning can survive – this is the culture of enquiry. The reflective space, as I described it earlier, takes the form of the 'culture of enquiry' in a therapeutic community.

Enquiry into the state of the community is equivalent to the characteristic attitude in psychoanalysis that enquires into the transference and countertransference. The analytic couple need continually to address the question: 'What is going on between us?' A therapeutic community, too, must enquire into its practices in the same way. As we have seen in this and the last chapters the community state veers from severe rigidity and ossification, as Main described, to fragmented disorganisation; but alternatively, a more flexible growth-enhancing state (Hinshelwood 1987a) may be attained. Therapeutically we seek that flexible, adaptable state of the institution which will reverberate therapeutically with the internal state of the individuals, countering their disintegration or rigidity. The same process of constant enquiry is the basis of the survival of an alive and healthy institution.

If teaching, knowledge and learning can be used by the next generation to avoid thought, feeling and the anxieties that accompany it, continuous enquiry about the hospital's structures, procedures and rituals is necessary for staff to remain open, as far as possible, to anxieties, however painful and conflictual, which need to be reflected on. The culture of enquiry is the maintenance system for servicing the reflective space.

If reflection is vulnerable to attack in the minds of individuals, then the community itself has to represent the drive to enquire, perhaps in the form of its timetabling of reflective events. A structural component of that kind can ensure the culture of enquiry whilst the members may be temporarily mentally maimed in this function. Institutional pressure for interpersonal reflection can enhance mutual support for each other amongst the staff and the patients. This may be effective when not all are directly caught up in an incident. More senior patients may be very active in this enquiry as well as trained staff.

I have turned, in this chapter, from the examination of the underlying problems to begin some thoughts on how to develop the practice at an institutional level. These thoughts dwelt on the culture of enquiry and the means to sustain it. This is the first step in answering the question at the beginning of the chapter – how to enhance reflection. However, the life of a community depends on much more than programmed events for enquiry and reflection. In the next chapter we will look at the possibility of therapeutic intervention in the broader aspects of community life.

Notes

1   These types are derived from Bion's later writings on groups in 1970. For a fuller treatment of these types of container in a therapeutic community, see Hinshelwood (1987), and for more details of these illustrations, see Hinshelwood (1994b).

2   This is a version of 'the institution in the mind' (Armstrong 1991), also described as the 'workplace within' (Hirschhorn 1995) or the institution's 'phantasy form and content' (Jaques [1953] 1955).

CHAPTER II

Reflection and Action

Despite claiming in my Introduction that this book would be inspired by psychoanalytic ideas, we have come to a point where we reach their limits. In certain respects, they are severely limited, limited to communication in the symbolic world of words. The therapeutic community is a practice that is beyond words, and has the potential to complement psychoanalysis with a theory of action. Psychoanalysis is very good at reflection and is perhaps the paradigm of a reflective practice. It opposes action to reflection and sets the two against each other. Relevant though this is to the psychoanalytic session where the golden rule applies (only to speak, and to do so without censoring the thoughts spoken), such a limitation is not helpful outside the psychoanalytic session, or related psychotherapies. The therapeutic community has been driven to move on beyond that limitation. I have begun the process of bringing reflection and action out of an opposition to each other, and to understand the ways in which they combine, complement each other, and to consider when, under some circumstances, they do oppose each other.

Surprisingly the therapeutic community has had to accomplish this largely on its own. Its nearest related cousin is group therapy, which on the whole accepts the psychoanalytic limitation of the 'golden rule'. It is all too easy then for a small field like the therapeutic community to be dominated by the ideas coming from group therapy, and thus to find itself unwittingly tied by limits imported from psychoanalysis. My plea is that the therapeutic community should promote its own unique contribution which is to transcend words, and to rediscover action as its prime therapeutic tool (see also Christian and Hinshelwood 1979).

Earlier, I described how a mind needs to have a space for reflection before acting in order to avoid acting-out its impulses (page 98), and a group needs to provide a firm interpersonal space of this kind for individuals who need to build up resources for reflection inside themselves. There are problems with developing an internal reflective space. Certain patients are particularly prone to use the reflective space as one to intrude into so that it becomes filled with impulsive action. For a large number of people, reflection cannot easily proceed to the stage of symbolic communication and words. The reasons for this are complex, technical, and not completely understood, and we will not dally with them here. It is merely a discovered fact that for many more disturbed patients it is the act of a coherent structure that is more telling than verbal discourse.[1] This is true of the expressive therapies, for instance where the structure of sound in music therapy (rhythm, melody, etc.) or the shaping of paint in art therapy (see Milner 1950) is as important as any content. Work may therefore be the most potent form of working through for people who are not very verbal in the first place. It can be particularly effective for everyone since the end-result is very concrete – a meal is cooked and community colleagues are fed and can be appreciative.

If we can combine reflection and enquiry with action, then we need to ask: how is such a practice actually performed? The unique feature of therapeutic community practice is to develop and sustain a non-verbal reflection, one that can be integrated with verbal reflection. Active and responsible work is the core of this practice.

Though many therapeutic communities have particular slots in the programme for the members to practice reflecting – being a witness of the community from a stance of involved separation, that third position (page 86) – the organisation is more than the content of those meetings. Longer-term benefit demands the internalisation of a coherent working organisation – an internalisation that lasts long after the person has left the community or institution. The internalisation needs to be a robust container that contains the patient, a step towards 'containing oneself'.

I stress in this book the therapeutic process as one of internalised coherent structure (see Chapter 8). Many patients who require institutional treatment respond to the *quality* of the organisation rather than to sophisticated thought. In assessing that quality of coherence, the kind of activity may well be a more telling measure. So, when it comes to a residential or communal setting, the coherent survival of the institution has a double benefit. It both ensures the institution continues to exist, and it also provides a paradigm of coherent organisation to be internalised by people with internally incoherent personalities. Hence, in Chapter 9, I began a theory of healthy action.

The institutional organisation depends on the more ordinary activities, the physical work on which life depends. This is purposeful action, which embodies a degree of reflection. The reflection consists of the thought that has gone into designing the action to meet the need. In these circumstances action has a thought-out purpose and is thus relatively healthy. Some action embodies reflection and some does not. We can set out clearly the kinds of actions we have been dealing with. It helps to think of two dimensions on which four kinds of action can then be plotted, as in Table 11.1. The two dimensions are: (a) that between impulsive or thoughtful (the dimension of disorder or therapeutic benefit); and (b) that between minds and material objects.[2]

Table 11.1 The relations between thought and action		
	Action on the material world	*Action on minds*
A – T (*Impulsive action without thought*)	1. Acting out	2. Intrusion
A + T (*'Healthy' action*)	3. Productive work	4. Communication

First, there is the impulsive, explosive action, maybe of a violent kind (page 104) or of the self-destructive kind (Maria, page 94).

Second, we have seen that though action is normally seen as physical behaviour, there is a definite action upon another mind. The action on another mind may be violently intrusive so that the other mind is taken over and functions mindlessly – as in the example of Maria again. But these are the impulsive forms of action – either on minds or on the material world (including the subject's own material body).

Third, we know that some action must be different from this, and forms the basis of life. This is productive action or work, and it carries with it the results of reflection; work-oriented action carries within it the knowledge of the task and how the particular action contributes to that task.

And *fourth,* to talk of the action of one mind on another implies a 'healthy' form of that 'action' – one which is not an invasion of another mind. That is, I think, what we would normally call communication (verbal or non-verbal) – the act of communicating reflection.

Action does not come to the fore in most psychotherapy. It is therefore the unique gift of the therapeutic community to offer this model of therapeutic needs. So, with some clarification of these kinds of action, we are in a position to explore the core principle of the therapeutic community.

Therapeutic community work

Physical tasks devoted to the material conditions must be performed in therapeutic communities as in any institutions. But typically in a therapeutic community, work on the material basis of life is the meaningful dimension of therapy. Work groups perform such tasks as shopping, cooking, cleaning, maintenance work and decorating, as well as those devoted to money-raising activities such as jumble sales, crafts for retailing, and so on. But the aim of the work in the community is to support healthy responsibility within the context of everyday life (Griffiths and Pringle 1997; James 1987; Kennedy 1987). The 'work of the day' comprises quite ordinary daily activities like cleaning the bedroom, but also significant responsibility such as helping to cook supper for all, to quite major responsibilities that include managing a work team (or a leisure activity), chairing meetings, caring for each other's well-being and providing a rota of support for those in crisis. Graduated levels of activity can be found for everyone. The detailed practice of working with patients to carry responsibility can be found in other works (Barnes *et al.* 1997; Clark 1964; Day and Pringle 2001; Griffiths and Pringle 1998; Jones 1968; Kennard 1983, 1999). As I stated in my Introduction, this is not a 'how to' manual for therapeutic communities, and I shall not go beyond these brief statements about the work – much greater detail can be found in the works cited. Instead I want to examine the psychological, sociological and political principles that lie behind therapeutic community thinking.

Work is important insofar as it touches on the responsibility to produce, and is seen as a form of non-verbal reflective communication and support. In a living institution, a vital dynamic between social demand and social refuge allows those within to reach a level of responsibility they can manage. A therapeutic community dissolves the division of labour, abolishing the helper–helpless dynamic, described by Main (page 45). Staff must also demand and patients can and do help and care. So the therapeutic community must hunt for, recognise and display that aspect of the humanity of every member, patient as well as staff, that is capable of care and devotion, as well as being cared for; that part of him that can acknowledge and work for something outside himself and bigger than himself. In traditional care, where the division of labour is rigid and exclusive, we saw at the start the disastrous decline of chronic patients as well as the institution itself.

Work is responsible action – action that gains meaning in terms of the material needs of oneself, colleagues and the institution. For containing those people whose actions tend to be acting-out, the important principle was stated in Chapter 9, that healthy action requires a reflective component. This does not have to be verbal reflection, since work aimed at providing for self and others is a reasoned message in itself. It might of course be possible to put it into words, say: 'If I cook, we all eat.' Or, 'If I don't cook, we don't eat' is an equally powerful implicit reasoning. But these words are not necessary for the message to be 'readable'. This is responsible action, it is meaningful work, it has consequences. Because there are real effects, and because others are significantly involved in the consequences, these implicit reflections have an added punch, which verbal therapy cannot so easily offer.

Responsibility and work

At the same time, such reflection on the consequences of action (even if not verbalised) creates a powerful experience that has itself to be contained. It is the experience of being responsible. Responsibility is often a critical area for people who need institutional care.[3] They often feel, intensely, not very good at the responsibility. Thus, an active form of treatment, that involves real work, touches on both the critical moment in a person's disturbance, his sense of responsibility and at the same time, an access to his crucial problem of reflection.

So many fragmented disturbed people suffer a burden of responsibility for themselves and for their impulses towards other people. They feel their personal resources have ebbed away with their fragmented selves, and their ability to put right what they think they may have done seems to them so puny. Much that is required from them seems to represent an overwhelming task. In the place of responsibility there looms failure and usually guilt. Psychoanalytically this scene is an internal one in which a harsh slave-driving conscience, or super-ego, berates the person, in an internal replica of an external abuse the person may have encountered in early life. The slightest failings mean failure, writ-large. The ferocity of their own expectations, coupled with their sense of depletion in themselves, is an explosive mixture. They break into states of mind and behaviour which is intolerable for everyone. Their worst fears of themselves are confirmed. A life of such circular defeat is frequently ended early and often brutally.

When demands feel heavy, responsibility is a powerful source of guilt. So that action which has consequences is close to the nub of individuals' problems. Usually as a result of aggression in his phantasy life, he experiences others as damaged by himself. Whilst people do in reality hurt each other, these phantasies tend to be of a very much greater degree of violence, and truly of a phantasy intensity. It can then be difficult for more disturbed people to sort out the reality of what they have done and what they have phantasised. Reassessing in a persistent (and in a sense courageous) way what is real and what is phantasy is the core support in a therapeutic community. It is support for the capacity to self-assess, to reflect on oneself. Maintaining that unique contribution of the therapeutic community is difficult, as it requires the knack of reflection in action as much as in words.

Sympathy and support

So, work must always be in the context of a supporting relationship. The patient and the staff work together on this in different roles. A patient can carry a lot of responsibility, provided he gets enough support. Staff work 'alongside'; that is to say, their work is to offer that support (Barnes *et al.* 1997; Griffiths and Hinshelwood 1997). The staff member does not care for the patient; instead he must support the patient to be a carer – to care for himself, for others, and to care for the job he does in the community. There are four main components to support:

1. to recognise the real responsibility, as distinct from phantasies which may far out-reach reality

2. to prompt solutions to the problems that are faced in the real situation

3. to assess the real accomplishment (or failure) during and after work has been completed

4. to help the patient to acquire this realistic self-assessment in the face of reality.

The staff member works with the patient on a job; he does not work *on* the patient. The supporting worker converts the patient's problems and issues at work, into questions of what to do, a review of possible solutions, and a testing of the reality that throws up the problem and the possible solutions.

New behaviour is explicitly demanded of patients. A substitute for the symptom is required. A patient might be addressed thus: 'I know you are feeling bad today, but you can still get through your work. Let me help you. Come along.' The substitute for the symptom – to be with others, to engage in whatever relation is possible, maybe to talk, but significantly to relate over meaningful action – is a significant message in its own right. It implies both an acknowledgement of distress – arising maybe from the work or the responsibility – and an acknowledgement of the worth of the person's contribution which cannot be lost. Such a message with the all the complex components is sophisticated indeed, despite not all being explicitly in words. The expectation is that turning to new relationships of support (eventually to be internalised) will gradually take the place of symptoms and dangerous behaviour. The support may be implicit, but no less thoughtful for that.

The community is thus a network of relationships for support and being supported. All patients are expected to play a part as both supporter and supported (and this is to some extent true of staff). The work of the day is thus one of a maximum degree of responsibility from a particular person, at a particular time, drawing on the support that is available everywhere.

Support to carry on the work of the day is relentless. Patients are encouraged to continue with their work, their catering, their management of their team, their chairmanship, etc. in the face of these crippling and unrealistic states of guilt and failure. If the work group is supported the feelings of guilt can turn from that crushing fear of punishment towards a more manageable sense of responsibility. Such a relief reduces the pressure to act-out. Instead, taking action can lead to internalising that reflective support. Psychoanalytically this represents a very concrete external support that the patient initially needs, and can then eventually internalise. The result aimed for is an internal support for a sense of personal well-being. This conceptualises how we can interrupt the cycles of abuse; it is through the intervention of a non-abusive supporter working alongside. This literal 'working through' does not focus directly upon pathology and symptoms, but demands and supports the functioning side of the person. It is a working through in action.

The therapeutic community stresses that therapeutic experiences arise from *actions*, as well as verbal interaction. Actions are important in a different way from words. They *directly* affect the quality of life of the community for good or bad, and this gives people's work full meaning. Basing the life of the community on the work and play of the patients involves a recognition by staff of the patients' active side, of allowing it to speak out. This strategy combats the view of patients as helpless and as wholly sick. It is crucial that all staff recognise that patients, however disturbed, are also capable of functioning in quite ordinary and helpful ways, even though these may be basic manual and non-verbal activities.

Diversions from work

Work places responsibility on patients who, often in fear of the responsibility and ensuing guilt, turn to outrage against these expectations put upon them. Under these sorts of pressures, patients develop their symptoms, depression, self-harm, hallucinations and paranoias. Or more articulately, they may hold that indeed they should not be pressured to make a contribution to their fellows. That resistance against an active life in the community does make some sort of sense. However, such sense is only superficial. The institution which makes no demands on the individuals for responsible action denies access to a critical issue for patients; it denies them opportunity to gain support when stressed by responsibility.

Members' attitudes towards work may subvert it as an authentic relation with others in various ways:

Subverting responsibility

In the common view, work towards the benefit of the community is unrewarding and boring. Work such as washing-up has been eloquently described by Holden (1972), who quotes one patient as saying, 'How can I be expected to do the washing-up? I feel so weak that I can't even do my own washing-up at home. I have had a complete breakdown, that's why I have come to the hospital. I need rest, I need to be looked after. I know that it has to be done – but why can't it be done by those who are able-bodied? I can't do it – if I could I wouldn't need to be here' (p.3). Members can feel exploited by the staff, whose job is supposed to be to organise things better – it is a hospital, after all (as was eventually asserted against Bion at Northfield, see page 48).

Staff carers

The subversion of action may be aggravated by professional attitudes to the 'real' work. All professionals wish to care, it is so often what they came into the work for. But unless it remains clear that care is not of the traditional kind, staff can become competitive with each other, often on interdisciplinary lines, for the available roles of care. Staff need to feel valued and important. To be seen to be effectively caring reassures many well-motivated staff. But this is just the kind of supportive satisfaction that patients need, and can be excluded from if the staff are too effective at keeping it to themselves. It is, as this kind of occurrence shows, very enhancing to be demanded of by someone dependent.

Dependency

The growth of the welfare state, the readiness of members of therapeutic communities to become dependent, and sometimes a confused ideology, have in conjunction allowed treatment to focus increasingly on therapy groups. Work has then come to refer, in therapeutic communities, to some internal operation, supposed to be under the control of a conscious will, as are the voluntary muscles. This is a retreat into reflection, leaving responsible action as therapeutically redundant, and a reversion to the opposition between reflection and action.

Collusion with narcissism

Though we could retain this contrast between internal work on the individual's intra-psychic processes and the external work that is meaningfully related to the 'community's needs', there is a danger. The danger is that internal work becomes a collusion with the narcissistic side of the individuals who seek to be in the centre of indulgent attention. In fact, in a group or community, in order to gain his own ends, an individual must devote himself to the ends of the community in which he will achieve his own ends. The individual, *with his internal states*, is a part of something that stretches far beyond him; he is part of something bigger than himself. It is in this sense that the therapeutic community is, and must be, a microcosm of real society. The treatment situation might then realise the subtle and difficult mixture of altruism and egoism that life is all about.

But making a contribution can often boil down to the question of who does the dirty work. The tack of 'you (the members) should do these domestic chores because it is good rehabilitation' is met by the member's answer that he expects to be doing bigger, better and more important work when he leaves. He says, 'You are wrong. Chores are not rehabilitation.' This can seduce certain staff into a collusive game with members over a search for the perfect job. As Meyer (1969) points out, 'this merely puts off the evil day when a compromise has to be made' (p.41). He described a girl who, like many emotionally deprived people, wanted to find 'work with animals. This is difficult to get, so she eventually compromised by working in a bird seed factory.' The unwillingness to make this kind of compromise may be reinforced by the attitude expressed by a member who said, 'It's the staff who do the real work.' And by the real work he meant the glamour of managerial meetings and responsibility. Patients are left the work that is unglamorous in the community value system, and the sense of contribution to colleagues is degraded into chores.

Internal work

As work groups have moved from social therapists and instructors in the early days of therapeutic communities to nurses and occupational therapists, professional training has focused the trainees' attention increasingly on the individual. This is the glamorous work. But the reality is that certain work tasks are necessary and urgent, without which the living conditions would decline below levels acceptable to a consensus of the community. It is only such tasks as these that can give work meaning in the community (Jones, Pomryn and Skellern 1956). Many therapeutic communities depend on the financial resources of funding bodies who expect most material needs to be met by the employment of paid cooks, cleaners and maintenance staff. It means that many pieces of work that are in fact within the capacities of members of the community are denied to them. So often the tasks remaining are the psychological ones of verbal therapy, thus catering for a more thoughtful, less manual, predominantly middle-class clientele, with higher education and with ambition to reach subsequent professional or managerial status (rather like the staff). Real work then means the clever stuff of interpreting, and being 'head-bound'. The whole treatment diverts into an extension of group therapy, and loses the unique opportunities of a therapeutic community.

Inauthentic work

Under pressures from these various factors, historically, over the years, the concept of work as a useful contribution has drifted away. Work has slipped from the prime focus of attention of most therapeutic communities. Instead it has suffered from one of, or some combination of, four other ideas:

1. something to occupy patients' time

2. something to enhance their personal confidence

3. physical activity is inferior to therapy activity

4. a notion of 'internal' work as superior to a contribution to the community.

Society versus the individual

My emphasis goes against the trend that has occurred ever since the anthropological analysis of the Henderson Hospital by Rapaport (1960). This stressed a view of the community as a social entity, which has been both fruitful and limiting. It is fruitful in sustaining the idea of the community to which the individuals both relate and belong – and this has sustained therapeutic communities over a period when in the wider culture social and cultural entities have tended to be ignored or denied in favour of the individual as the sole focus of interest. It has been limiting in that, taking a social perspective, the psychology of the individual has become submerged in the general principles of the social running of a community. Rapaport's principles – permissiveness, communalism, democratisation and reality-confrontation – amount to a political programme; they imply respect for the individual, but are naive about individual psychology. This cannot be rectified by adding a therapeutic focus on the individual.

The therapeutic community is a sophisticated political programme, and has gained influence, and has often inspired humane residential care in the field of psychiatry. Nevertheless, without a detailed examination of the relations between the institution and the individual level, it does not go as far as it might, as I have repeatedly emphasised. All the same, much has been gained by the promotion of therapeutic community principles over the decades. What is needed is a fulcrum around which both the political programme of the community and the individual psychology of patients can spin together. I claim that fulcrum is the painful experience of individual responsibility for work in the community.

Working through in the therapeutic community

In therapeutic communities, or any mental healthcare institution, work needs to be seen as coming to terms with damage for which one feels responsible – the damage a patient has made of his life, his body and his many past relationships. The working-through process is to engage with the tough side of work, the tough internal conditions necessary for 'doing work' – that is, the tough experience of facing damage and responsibility for it. Nowhere are the problems of responsibility more obvious, or more directly reached therapeutically, than in, say, cooking for the community meal. This internal work on responsibility is enhanced and supported by the staff's capacity to think and reflect on the patient's position and his burdensome, crushing, responsibility. This encourages the patient to focus on it too through the concrete work.

But equally so, staff must work through the damage done to patients – either in their phantasies, or in the actuality of the damaging effects of psychiatric services and institutions. This ever-present risk of damage has to be continuously worked through. And we have now come full circle. As Denis Martin wrote in the quote at the beginning of this book: '…the patient, resigned and co-operative…too passive to present any problem of management, has in the process of necessity lost much of his individuality and initiative' (Martin 1955, p.1190). The damage wrought on the patients' personalities by the staff and their institutions is precisely a damage to the patients' capacities for responsibility and active initiative. With the arrival at the importance of responsible work in a therapeutic community, we have taken a journey beneath the many other descriptions of institutionalisation. And the key – the problem of responsibility as a pressure and burden which can dismantle actual thought – can be as usefully addressed in activity relations with others as in verbal forms of therapy.

There is therefore a joint process to be engaged in by patients and staff. The work of the therapeutic community in joining the reflective task with the level of action and responsibility makes work and working through converge.

Notes

1   It is, of course, true that verbal discourse is itself highly structured and organised. However, even with the relatively sophisticated patients who present for a psychoanalysis, it is now well known the coherence and consistency of the organisation (daily sessions, clear time-boundaries, etc.) is also very important. The analysand reacts to that structure and rhythm, and much verbal analysing is devoted to an awareness of their impact and deviations.

2   This is the significant dimension in a psychoanalysis, where movement from action in the material world to action in the mental world is required.

3   And indeed for all persons seeking treatment however mild their symptoms – this principle of responsibility is enshrined in the psychoanalytic technical term, 'depressive position'.

PART III

Relational Networks

Introduction to Part III

In Part II, we developed an extensive theory of institutional functioning, with special reference to the therapeutic community. The emphasis has been to try to avoid merely an individual psychology, and also to resist simply a sociological perspective. Instead, Part II commenced with an attempt to grasp the experience and phenomenology of the individual *in* the institution. That led to significant ways of understanding what can be therapeutic about the institution. I pinpointed the boundary between impulsive action and communication/production as the key area to focus on. In Part III I want to develop this as a theory of institutions in general, although it will remain grounded in the experience of mental health institutions. It means moving on at times from specifically mental health practice.

The intrusive and communicative methods of impacting on another person's mind depend on the extraordinary mechanisms of the mind that are known as splitting projection and introjection. They are often the core feature of pathological states as discovered by psychoanalysis. But I have been showing that they are not restricted to pathology, and in fact the boundary between pathology and normality is more or less unsustainable – staff as well as patients are involved alike in these projective systems. And, as I have stressed all the way through, it is best to jettison those conventional notions of pathology, which assign normality to some and pathology to others in malfunctioning institutions.

It might be helpful, as an aside at this point, to describe this dimension – along which both patients and staff can slide. That dimension defines the phenomena of impulsiveness versus communication/production. At one end, projective process can have a quite benign quality. In fact, projection is a common feature of personal interactions – perhaps the very basis of relationships (Heimann 1952). In greeting someone, a smile will create a comfortable sense in the other person of being someone pleasant to meet, a good person. Alternatively, people may project unpleasant states – a frown, for instance, has the opposite effect of a smile. For instance, we might say that 'A' gives 'B' a piece of her mind – by this we mean that 'A' is angry with 'B', knows she is angry with 'B' and intends that 'B' will actually feel inside him something of that anger. However, in another process 'A' may provoke 'B' to anger, by making 'innocent-sounding' remarks: 'Oh, darling, I have a headache tonight', for example. Then an initial state in 'A', an anger that gives her a headache, is transported into 'B' rejecting her. And here 'A's' mental state is lost from her, whilst 'B' gains a state of disturbance (see Hinshelwood 1995).

Frequently blame is projected into others, often forcefully. For example, after two people crash into each other in their cars, there is a typical scene in which the drivers leap out and throw accusations at each other. The *throwing* of accusations conveys a physical transferring of something towards the other with violence. We know blame is psychic and is not a physical substance; however, it can be pictured, even felt, in physical terms – and indeed sometimes the drivers may end up throwing actual physical things at each other, for example their punches.

People look to each other in this way to put across their troubles, to find a sympathetic ear. And society's institutions are available for people to use for modifying their distress through the contact with others (Jaques 1955). With funerals, for instance, it is the 'I know how you feel' response which is looked for. And 'knowing' means more than having the dictionary definition – instead it means actually feeling *for* the other person, so that both can feel it. This is the other end of the dimension, when both can have a feeling. It is at the opposite end from the impulsive, intrusive and explosive kind of projective impact on another mind. One loses what the other gains.

The chapters in Part III concern the way emotional states, normally associated with individual consciousness, can move step by step through the institutional dimension. Mental states unthinkingly are exported (by projective processes) from person to person in an institution – even amongst quite 'normal' people. The individual exists in a network of personally felt relations, through which disturbance can be transported, and that relational network forms a kind of institutional container. This is exemplified in each of the chapters, and the sequence of emotional links between persons can be followed. The translation of this form of emotional transport into an alternative form, the communication of meaning, uses words and reflection, but can also be mediated by actions. More extended sequences can be seen to underlie institutional behaviours and culture. Here the process of sequencing unthought psychic actions upon one another occurs amongst quite ordinary people, who export quite ordinary disturbances between themselves; each one 'feels' the disturbance in their own way, and becomes unthinkingly locked into the sequencing.

CHAPTER 12

A Group as Network

How actually do the individuals relate in the process of 'being' the institution? In an earlier illustration where linking occurred (see page 102), a small group session appeared to generate a space for the appreciation of one another beyond the cognitive meanings (the reflective space). That session showed us an emotional progression as something in one person proceeds to affect another. There is a kind of containment going on, a reflective linking at an emotional level, not just at the cognitive level, nor was it necessarily conscious either – an emotional link as if the receiving person has been affected by the emotional tone carried from the speaker before. In that chapter, I detailed the vicissitudes of linking in groups (pages 102–108), and compared that group session with another where linking did not seem to happen at that emotional level. I now move on from that containing culture (or atmosphere) of a group to another feature. That is a sequential process that goes on in these cultures. I shall start by once again turning to a small therapeutic group, because the events that occur remain largely within a space which remains observable. In larger institutions which we will come to later, it is increasingly difficult to capture detailed processes because this so rapidly extends beyond reach for any one observer.

The following example is a group where an unconscious rapport amongst the members occurred. This example shows a sequence of linking from one person to another, to a third. We can almost 'see' something being passed around the network of the group. The emotional tone, affecting one and then another and another, appears to travel through the network like the ball on a pinball table. There are five people in this group. Previously, two members had dropped out prematurely, leaving the group feeling guilty that they had not done more to keep the other two.

Mrs A was known to be in difficulties with her marriage. Her husband had grown more and more critical of her over the years and she was anxious about her future and how she could continue to bring up her two young children. She began the group by telling a story about a bus conductor who refused to let her enter. Mrs A talked as if to no one in particular and tended to irritate the other members by this impersonal manner of dominating the group. It was as if no one else got a chance to come in on the monologue. Eventually Mr B interrupted her. He is a quiet man who the group knew to be an adopted child and who was trying to find his own (biological) mother. Painfully, he told a familiar story about his girlfriend who, the group already knew, went out with other men. There was a palpable relief amongst the members that Mrs A had been stopped, but a sort of boredom with Mr B developed. At this point the therapist, intending to do something about the flat, bored tone that had come over the group, confronted the group with the way Mrs A dominated the dialogue and how Mr B had come in to stop it.

The therapist, in describing Mrs A's dominating behaviour, did not properly address the complete process and as a result the group went on in an atmosphere as if they had been criticised by his comments.

Mr B turned to Mrs C, a depressed woman who has a poor relationship with her mother, and asked if they were getting on any better. Mrs C once again told the group the story that her mother wanted grandchildren and Mrs C had not yet been able to produce any. She began to shed tears.

In this sequence Mrs A had irritated the other members of the group, but it seemed that unconsciously she may have been expressing her chilling experience (losing her marriage and her home) through the story of being excluded from the bus. This had affected Mr B, the adopted child, who acted on behalf of the others to try to deal with Mrs A's monopolising talk. One could say that Mr B experienced feeling left out by Mrs A in a way that was analogous to Mrs A's feeling left out at the bus stop, and, probably, this touched on his own experience of being excluded (given for adoption) by his own mother. So Mr B was provoked to do something. He talked about his own trouble – with his girlfriend. Then Mr B managed the group by bringing in Mrs C, probably unconsciously. He did so for a purpose; she also represented the experience of being out of favour and excluded from a desired maternal approval.

There are various ways in which this material could be understood, but I am trying to draw attention to the way a *state of feeling* is passed around the network of members. This particular state of feeling seemed to be one of exclusion from a home or from a state of approval or affection (which is what a home means emotionally).

Mrs A's sense of losing her marriage and maybe her home and children was expressed in the story of being excluded from the bus. But it was also expressed in a different mode, and this is the important occurrence that I am trying to describe. By her impersonal and dominating mode of talking she made this *state of mind* (feeling excluded) actually occur in the other members of the group, especially Mr B. He too told a story about being excluded (by his girlfriend), but in the process of talking about it, he also did something to the rest of the group. The boredom provoked the therapist to try an interpretation, probably rather prematurely. The therapist tried to come in, as it were, but to no avail; he was ignored and felt left out. Finally, Mr B, still full presumably of his own experience with his girlfriend, brought out in Mrs C a similar feeling, the maternal disapproval. A feeling state was passed from member to member – Mrs A to Mr B, to the therapist, to Mr B again, and to Mrs C – and each gave that state his or her own embellishments, and responded with his or her own particular 'business'; but the emotional state mobilised one person after another in a chain reaction.

Foulkes' idea of the interpersonal matrix similarly situates the individual at the nodal points of an inter-communicational network (Foulkes 1975; Roberts 1982). Foulkes' term to describe this linking up was 'mirroring'. And he described chain reactions in small therapeutic groups (Foulkes and Anthony 1957). He never took these observations much further, and certainly not in the direction in which I am interested (though he did relate the phenomenon to something he called the condenser effect – a kind of group catharsis). Foulkes' matrix tends to be realised (and encouraged) as free-floating discussion of conscious meanings, meanings which to be sure have an unconscious depth. Foulkes wrote little about institutional processes, partly because he was primarily interested in group therapy of the individual, and because he was focused more on the ego than the unconscious, paying attention to conscious verbalised themes that reverberated in the group. For this reason, I claim that the observations here go beyond Foulkes' work in this respect.

I am taking a slightly different perspective. It is a perspective from the level of the unconscious linking-up process. To be sure the process has a conscious expression in verbalised meanings, words and roles, but it is the deeper, emotional impact embedded within the words which is important. If we answer the question at the beginning of this chapter about how people 'are' the institution, I am directing attention to the way that individuals impact on one another in the course of being together. People, as we have seen, make an impact – they do not just pass information. I specifically draw attention to the *sequential* nature of *repeated resonances* that go around the group. This linking process between people may relate to what LeBon (1895) called 'contagion', in which some emotion spreads like an epidemic around a group or crowd. Coherent meanings and significances may emerge, but the responses are linked together by the unconscious similarities in the emotions, the affective tone. I wish to pursue this kind of chained sequence as if some emotional 'particle' were moved in an identifiable track through the network of listeners in the group. We will look at this in the institutional setting, in the next chapter, and illustrate this chain phenomenon with one occurrence on one occasion in a mental health setting.

CHAPTER 13

The Supervision Network

I want now to address the question whether these sequential network occurrences can be observed in the wider setting of the institution rather than just the circumscribed entity of a small group. And if they can, what relevance are they to our investigation of institutional functioning? The following example does confirm that serial impacts on individual emotional states do operate on the wider scale. In this example, a series of emotional impacts took place in a large mental hospital, tracing a path through the existing relational network.

The following describes the passage of something very disturbing through a part of the institution (this material was first published in Hinshelwood 1987b, pp.269–270). It seems it was sexual, arising between patients, and led to a particular impact on one of the nurses. She in turn took her own anxious and defensive state to someone for support and/or supervision.

The charge nurse, Cath, phoned to ask if I would help her by discussing a patient she had been seeing for weekly counselling. She explained that she felt concerned about what she was trying to do and out of her depth working with a chronic schizophrenic who was not improving.

When she arrived, Cath came with one of her staff nurses, a woman I had not met before, who remained mostly silent. We discussed the patient. Margaret was a chronic schizophrenic, who had originally been admitted to the hospital many years ago. Cath complained that, though Margaret had been successfully rehabilitated to live in a group home, a few months ago she had got herself readmitted to the rehabilitation ward in the hospital. This seemed to Cath to be a manipulation. What particularly frustrated Cath was that Margaret could manage practical things perfectly well, she could behave and talk quite rationally; but there was a completely different side to her which was sad and hallucinated, and concentrated on delusions about wires. Cath was exasperated by this contradiction and the problem of getting her back to life in a group home which she was quite able to manage practically.

We discussed a little of what had gone wrong. Margaret had claimed that she 'felt exposed' in the home. I asked about the amount of staff cover, and whether it was because she had no member of staff to turn to with her hallucinations etc. in the home. But, it seemed, she never did turn to staff anyway, even in hospital. There was some talk of her psychotic symptoms, which included hearing voices, and something about wires.

I asked what the wires were, and Cath told me about the patient's husband, who as time went on had grown apart from the patient in hospital, and had eventually divorced her, and remarried. The patient still felt bitter about that, but the husband provided a small allowance and gave presents at Christmas and for her birthday.

I pointed out that Cath had not answered a question about the wires. Her eyes turned downwards to the floor and, rather coyly, she said that Margaret believed that men were putting steel wires or springs into her vagina. When I said this referred to Margaret's sexual feelings, Cath could understand that, and seemed relieved to talk about it. She described how Margaret would often not sit properly on her chair but on her hands as if trying to make her bottom more comfortable. Cath also described with excited exasperation how in one of the counselling sessions with Cath, Margaret had said she was being bounced up and down by the men. Cath had argued this out with the patient in an amused way, asking Margaret if she could see herself bouncing up and down. When Margaret admitted 'no', but still continued to maintain that she was being bounced up and down, Cath felt even more exasperated.

I considered what I could do for Cath and noticed how I was struggling to give her something useful. It had been some immediate relief to discuss the sexuality; and I realised the staff nurse had been invited along (unconsciously) as a kind of chaperone! I said to Cath that Margaret might feel a relief if she could talk in the counselling about her own sexual feelings, as she probably had never had the chance in all her decades at the hospital. I conveyed, too, the limited possibilities of counselling a schizophrenic. However, what we had discussed made sense to Cath and she felt that she had got some good advice.

Yet I still felt bothered. Something was still not really understood. I found myself wanting to show off more of my ability to Cath. I clearly wanted to impress this attractive woman. My thoughts turned to the sexuality. I wondered why the situation at the group home had been untenable for Margaret. I was puzzled, too, by Cath's apparent coyness – she was a rather robust woman, married, and with a confident presence, and an evident sexual attractiveness. She had previously seemed a very open and physical woman. It seemed natural to pursue this theme. I wondered about sex at the group home and asked Cath whether the home had both men and women; and, if so, this might have affected Margaret. Cath suddenly sat back in her chair with her hand over her mouth with surprise and recognition. She exclaimed that I must know a certain patient who had been well known around the hospital as a 'flasher' and who 'masturbated all over the place'. He too had gone to the home at the same time as Margaret. So it was suddenly clear that Margaret 'felt exposed' because she lived in a house where a man regularly exposed himself. Cath could see this and felt greatly relieved.

In addition she and her staff nurse suddenly realised that Margaret is now resident, back in the hospital, in a room on the top floor of the ward block where she is the only woman. In fact there had been some fuss from her recently about changing her room.

We could talk further about sexuality. There had been an occasion when a student had been upset at finding Margaret lying on her bed with her legs apart in a very suggestive manner. Margaret often described her delusional bodily sensations as something which she had tried to resist. When asked why she did not try to resist them, and occupy herself with a useful practical programme, she said that she had been fighting them for years and now only wanted to give in to the sensations. It sounded, we agreed, like a phantasy of rape. And the supervision ran on in a much more relaxed way.

The upshot of this was that although Cath had come to talk about the counselling with Margaret, it had become more important to pay attention to the social milieu in which Margaret's symptoms emerged – in particular, the room allocation could be much more important than anything said in the counselling sessions.

The reflective space as process

The dynamics of the incident are important and unusually clear. A sequence of relationships had become mobilised one after another: (1) in the house, the 'flasher' had stirred and disturbed Margaret; (2) in the ward, Margaret had disturbed and frustrated nurse Cath; and (3) in the supervision, nurse Cath had engaged myself in a supervision which started tense, sexual and mystifying. A psychic 'substance', as it were, passed through the relationships in that order. Later (4) in the relationship between myself and Cath, the anxiety became strikingly modified by a moment of understanding. Finally, the modified distress could be converted back to action by (5) nurse Cath reorganising Margaret's room allocation.

Margaret had been exposed to sexual stimulation (probably only visual) which gave rise to bodily sensations and frustration. The schizophrenic form of psychic functioning *discharged* (projected) this stimulation in the form of delusions;[1] but thereby inserted a despairing anxiety into others, in this case the receptive nursing staff.

The intrusions into Margaret were experienced by her as violent – a rape – and their discharge into staff (and no doubt others on the ward) probably felt equally violent and disturbing. So much so that Cath came to me in desperation for some supervision and with an embarrassment that was odd in view of her confidence and her own apparent sexuality. With the patient, Cath had introjected an urgency that made Cath feel in need of protection and she had brought her 'chaperone' with her, the silent staff nurse.

In the consultation Cath put into me a good deal of urgency and the sense of helpless bewilderment, but in the course of being able to reflect on this together, there was a sudden moment of understanding from which Cath gained a feeling of support and a renewed confidence to go back to her work. A moment of understanding modified the anxiety for Cath and gave her a new sense of being able to face it, and to think in a new way about nursing Margaret.

In this sequence, we see Margaret's uncontained and intolerable emotional experience coming to be contained. She could not contain her own experience within a normal boundary. Typically for a schizophrenic patient she had channelled that disturbing experience into bizarre phenomena we call symptoms, and managed in that way to communicate her disturbance very well, by disturbing others with the same futile quality of uncontained meaning. The disturbance came free, as it were, and lost its moorings, to begin to roam through the network of personal relations in her immediate neighbourhood of the institution. We can see how there is a lack of reflection, an incapacity for reflection in the 'flasher' and in Margaret. Thought was also difficult for Cath, but she had some inkling how to augment her own capacities by asking for supervision. In the relations with her consultant psychotherapist (myself) the whole experience was raised to one for reflection.

This demonstrates the move from one kind of containment (by exporting to others, without thought, A – T) to a more mature one – reflection (A + T). The social context deals with the anxiety in one of two possible ways. They are distinguished by the degree to which meaning is given or taken away from the experience. When Cath brought her anxiety and the sense of its unknowableness to a supervision, the distance from the immediate impact of the anxiety on the ward allowed a space into which the anxiety could be opened up to scrutiny. In this case the bewilderment and frustration could be allowed time for acknowledgement and, with reflection, given a meaning.

In this case study, through enhancing the personality resources of the nurse, by giving space for her to reflect upon a state of mind received from a patient, the patient's psychotic symptoms became understandable. She could understand the meaning of the room allocation and the mix of patients in the wards and in the home. She could then begin to find ways to 're-project' back to Margaret an understanding in a suitable form. In this case, with a very chronic schizophrenic woman, it was not a verbal form but one which was in the form of an action. Dealing with new room allocations, for instance, was a form of communicating the reflection we had done, in a *language of actions*. And it may be that it is a form that is more appropriate for the schizophrenic. As I have suggested, some persons are only contained by actions – for instance the infant before speech has developed. Perhaps we can only communicate with those who are sufficiently disturbed to need in-patient admission by the action of admitting them. In a reflective therapy, understanding at the practical level of choices and action is as important as the understanding in words. So, an adequate social therapeutic milieu could be seen as a *relationship network* that accepts anxiety and distress, and can contain it, through reflection, by giving it meaning. That, in turn, gives the patient a chance to introject a capacity for greater understanding of their own intolerable experiences. I have described (Chapters 10 and 11) how important it is for the system to have a 'reflective space' built in for this function of containing and modifying anxiety (Hinshelwood 1979b). In contrast, systems which are not structured to give that kind of containing space leave incomprehensible symptoms unattended.[2]

Cath needed to attain a distance whilst also recognising her involvement. That important stance, the witnessing stance (see page 84), is hard for staff in all institutions. The capacity to reflect entails achieving a psychic distance. In the process, symbols, especially verbal symbols, are often the most important vehicle for reflection. However, 'reflection in actions' is crucial in many instances, as in Cath's revision of the room allocations. By reallocating Margaret a room, Cath was indicating a whole process of reflection, from which Margaret could (if able) take a sense of being understood. The capacity to move flexibly from words to actions as the means of reflection and communication is an important one for those working with severely disturbed people, especially in institutions.

Projection as an institutional process

The example just given illustrated projective processes, in which one person's internal world, or state of mind, affects others'. Although this is presented as a process arising in the horror of schizophrenic experience, it is not uncommon – as we have seen in group therapy. In more ordinary communication, projection operates as a common feature of personal relationships. And perhaps it is the very basis of relationships, as Heimann described (see page 128, above). People actively put emotions into others' minds as well as conscious ideas, cognitive contents, and information. People look to each other in this way to put across their troubles, with impact.

In the illustration, we were concerned with the conversion of psychotic experience, by more mentally robust individuals, into some sort of meaningful understanding. The experiences that more disturbed people have frighten others through the intensity of their projection, often so extreme the family ejects the culprit to a distance that lessens the impact of those projections. Families protect themselves from a kind of psychic assault, this intrusive, explosive action upon their minds. But then these concentrate in a psychiatric institution, as we have seen, to become a social milieu of routinised projections.

The example of Margaret is of interest in one other way. The work I did with Cath was a supervision. It suggests supervision is a kind of emotional exchange system (Hinshelwood 1979b) in which issues in the professional work arouse concerns in the worker, who tends to off-load to a greater or lesser degree to a supervisor. There is here a serial exchange between three people: patient to staff to supervisor. And the supervisor's role is to be a setting which can in some way take the anxiety and do some thinking about it. This is the creation of a reflective space, the purpose of which is to convert something anxious into something communicated. Then that something, reflected upon and now more meaningful, can be passed back down the chain. In such an instance, institutional life is working in a relatively ordinary and benign way. The occurrences in which states of mind are being projectively 'lost' in the system, as Margaret's might have been, is replaced by added bits of meaningfulness that could retrace the steps of the lost bit of emotion. Here is the beginning of an idea of what useful or healthy institutional functioning might be like at the level we are interested in – in other words, a working reflective space of an institution.

In answer to our starting point in this chapter about the relevance these chains of projections and impacts have for therapeutic institutions, we have seen a quite far-reaching reply. These interactions occur with all degrees of intensity from explosive intrusion to ordinary conversational impact. But specifically, in professional work, it could be a useful model for understanding and taking advantage of underlying dynamics in the supervisory relationship.

In the next chapter, we shall examine these instances of projective chains much further.

Notes

1   This is a characteristic response to unbearable experiences for many schizophrenics; and it contrasts with the method used by severe personality disordered people. Schizophrenic people emanate a rather cold, futile and despairing feeling, whereas personality disorders employ an explosive intrusion into another person's mind, as we saw in Chapter 9, that is a characteristic kind of excited dumping (see also Hinshelwood 1999b).

2   See also Murray Jackson's remarkable series of interviews which give 'space' for schizophrenic patients to explore their symptoms with him (Jackson and Williams 1994).

CHAPTER 14

Chains of Links

Although institutions are normally regarded as consciously formed collections of people and roles, with a socially assigned task, we have begun to explore another perspective in the last couple of chapters. What conclusions could be drawn if we consider an institution to be a social network that carries chains of serial projections through the relationships between individuals? In this chapter we will attempt to draw some of these conclusions.

The projective processes involved in these sequences are associated with two alternate states of mind; one is when there seems to be some obstruction to reflecting on it – there is in effect some hindrance of meaning and the state of mind remains incomprehensible. This was the state in which Cath presented herself initially in the example in the last chapter. In the other state of mind there was comprehension, a sense of emerging meaning – for instance, that 'eureka' moment when Cath, her staff nurse and I realised the immediate significance of Margaret's room allocation. The initial state of incomprehension evaporated and Cath's mind (as well as my mind) filled with a new meaning.[1]

These states of mind were occupied by people who were normally functioning, the nurse and myself, and not diagnosed as mentally ill. Clearly these processes are of great significance potentially for an institution dealing with incomprehensible madness, and especially when that 'madness' gets out of the patients and into the staff. In the institution, 'something' leaves the individual and embarks on a career as an institutional process. Though this example comes from a mental health institution, my sense is that we could generalise and say these processes play a part in more ordinary institutions; and it is true, in the next illustration, that the process occurs entirely within the staff of the unit. And indeed it originated with a disturbance that was not at all of the same mind-disrupting intensity as Margaret's. It did not have the desperate quality of incomprehension and was not so clearly in need of therapeutic conversion. Instead, in this example, a quite different institutional conversion occurred, a conversion from disturbance felt by individuals, to become an institutional outcome, an activity of the institution itself.

Institutional conversion

This illustration comes from a small clinic which contained a number of facilities for psychiatric and psychotherapeutic treatments, including an adult day hospital run along therapeutic community lines; a children's department which also ran a daily treatment programme for autistic children; and a weekly day-long 'school group' for primary school children who were disturbed. The staff worked in a highly democratised team, with a good deal of overlap between the departments. The social system was somewhat unusual for psychiatric institutions and a great deal of traditional authority was passed over to multidisciplinary meetings.

This example can be described as a number of steps, each one is a relationship in which one person passes on to another a piece of experience, like a hot potato (this illustration was first published in Hinshelwood 1982, pp.470–471). The notion of sequences of projection was elaborated further in Hinshelwood (1989c).

1. One morning Dr A arrived in the hospital building and found that the room she normally used was occupied by Dr B, a new locum.

2. Dr A was annoyed with the newcomer but, unable to interrupt Dr B who was interviewing a patient, she tackled the receptionist, Mrs C, blaming her for directing Dr B to the disputed room.

3. Mrs C was put in a bad humour. Now Dr A's ten year old son, D, was away from school that day and she had brought him to the hospital. Mrs C displaced her anger when Dr A was not present from the mother to the son, D. Mrs C criticised D, but he remained unabashed and disobliging.

4. Mrs C then made an accusation about D to Miss E. Miss E is one of the clinical staff and therefore has some responsibility to see that the behaviour of patients within the hospital remained within limits. In effect this was an attempt by Mrs C to activate the authority structure. Clearly it was easier for the receptionist to do this over D, a child, than over Dr A.

5. However, Miss E attempted to calm the situation by speaking to Dr A about her son D. But since the trouble had arisen over Dr B this discussion seemed irrelevant to Dr A. So Miss E's efforts in this direction came to nothing.

6. She tried again. This time Miss E pursued the authority structure by informing Dr F, the consultant with overall responsibility. She said D had annoyed Mrs C.

7. Dr F considered the problem. In his opinion, the most troublesome children in the hospital were those who attended the weekly 'school group' for children with severe behaviour disturbances. They constituted something of a problem for him. He decided that Mrs C's irritation was really derived from these children. Dr F conveyed his anxiety about controlling this 'school group' to the weekly staff meeting which functioned as the final authority in the hospital.

8. The staff meeting discussed this and became concerned about the impact of the children in the hospital as a whole. In particular it was thought that there may be friction between the adult patients and the children, and adults had often expressed anxiety about the special group of autistic children (quite different from the 'school group').

9. The staff meeting resolved that Miss G, the psychotherapist in charge of the Autistic Unit, should give a talk to the adult

Table 14.1 Steps in affect transformation	
Relationship	*Transformation*
1. Dr A – Dr B	Rivalry
2. Dr A – Mrs C	Argument
3. Mrs C – D	Complaint
4. Mrs C – Miss E	Alerting the authority system
5. Miss E – Dr A	Conciliatory attempt
6. Miss E – Dr F	Moving up the authority system
7. Dr F – Staff Meeting	Problem-defining
8. Staff Meeting – Miss G	Decision-making
9. Miss G – Day Patients	Action taken

patients about the children in her unit. The end result of the activation of the authority structure was action.

Affect flow

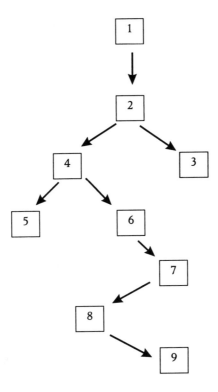

Figure 14.1 Flow chart of personal affect

Figure 14.1 is a flow chart to visualise how something arises in the social network, flows through formal and informal channels and ends up at a point far removed from the source.

There is a flow of personal affect which takes place in a specific medium, the series of relationships; and the diagram is a chain of them. The chain has two dead ends (3 and 5) in its flow through the relationship network of this social system.

What starts out as personal affect between two individuals ends up as something quite different. The origin is the strong affect in Relationship 1 – rivalry and anger. However, when we come to Relationship 9, it is very different; the content is a professional decision about a therapeutic action. The end-result is an action in the purpose of the institution. A major overall transformation has taken place; a sum of all the individual transformations from one relationship to the next. Although these transformations have an emotional impact, their significance is transitory. However, over the whole sequence, something significant has happened for the institution. An origin that was relatively trivial has turned into something task-oriented and purposeful. That overall transformation from minor personal affect to institutional purpose looks bizarre on the face of it. One can only smile that the action taken at the end is so distant from the inflamed tempers of A and C at the start. But, for the institution, some sort of energy has come into the organisation which prompted activity useful in its own right to the hospital. There is here an important linking process between personal meaning and institutional task. The purpose of the institution comes to be linked onto the energy of the relationships between the individuals. Something that was once personal and individual has become an asset of the institution that can drive useful task activity. This suggests that informal personal relationships do not just live alongside the formal structure but feed into it in an unexpected though significant way. The organisation gains its energy from the personal affects of the individual members.

This is an *institutional* transformation. It would appear that the formal structure has something to do with this linking of the personal into the institutional. It is a kind of accumulator, perhaps, that gathers energy for the organisational system. The energetic process is a driver of the dead, unmotivated and reified structure. Though the formal authority structure of roles, functions, tasks, employment contracts, etc. is designed for the primary institutional purpose, to come alive the institution must attract into itself the emotional liveliness of the individuals.

Alienation

The expropriation of the particle of experience comes about through transformations at each nodal point of the network. Each node, a person, takes in the particle and then gives it out. The individual actually loses some of his or her experience as it passes away through the ramifications of the network, and with it loses some of his or her own self. A split piece of experience comes adrift from one member and is projected as if it were a package, a discrete quantum of experience;[2] and this is based on individual mechanisms inside the person. These involve splitting, with feelings and relations being cut off from one another (Klein 1946), and projection of those split-off parts of the person. Because these primitive mechanisms are unconscious, the individual's investment in the institution at this level is equally unconscious. The loss to the person is nevertheless experienced in some way; and the institution is felt to be depersonalising. It comes to be felt as alien, split from the individuals who make it up. 'Faceless bureaucracy' or the 'monolithic organisation' are terms we use to convey the way institutions reduce the sense of identity of the individual. The mechanism of projection at the individual level becomes *alienation* at the level of the institution (Hinshelwood 1983).

The individual's personal experiences become depersonalised within the institution which, to an extent, *is* him. The institution is him in the sense that its energy has transformed from his personal being to an institutional resource, and he becomes raw material for the developing group culture and activity. The process binds the individual into an identification from which he has great difficulty in extricating himself whole. The individual's feeling states and experiences become 'commodities', reified bits of him, estranged from their source in him. And going back to the example of Margaret and Cath, in the last chapter, this reification and estrangement is surely a significant element of the phenomenon we started with, institutionalisation.

In the unconscious mind, parts of the individual members can be taken in and given out. Bits of identity are strewn through the institution as if they are as concrete and physical as dismembered parts of the body. This connects with the experience which I have described of the very concrete identification with the primary institution, the parents' bodies. That we called an identification by equation. It was the first of those levels of identification described in Chapter 7 (page 84), and this material shows that level of early or primitive experience, brought out in an institution. Adults are still prone to these infantile processes. And, moreover, it appears to be the case that it is a necessary condition for an institution to have a life. We must have available, even as adults, this capacity to engage as an infant does; our institutions depend on it.

Once again we need to notice that these processes occur in people who are in general mentally 'normal', and are not psychotic patients with whom this kind of disturbed identity is more commonly associated. This level of disturbance of mental function of quite ordinary people has been recognised for a long time. LeBon (1895) noted how the individual is reduced, in 'crowd psychology' as he called it, to levels of functioning well below that at which one is capable when alone.

One implication of this is that individuals in institutions for the care of the mentally ill have difficulty in sustaining their maximum maturity of functioning. They descend to a level in which minds operate without adequate reflection and interfere with each other in a way that, in the long run, breeds incomprehension. Indeed their minds become so geographically remote from their projected experience, any direct reflection on it becomes impossible. It appears that 'normal' mental health needs to be reconsidered. It is not that 'normal' people are immune from projective processes in which identities are distorted and confused. It is rather that, on the whole, they find it easier to recover themselves readily when they physically (or emotionally) remove themselves from the institutional projective system.

The goal of our journey

We have now reformulated the depersonalisation and alienation in the old institutions as the complexity of projective processes in the relational network. In these last two chapters, I described specific processes by which energetic parts of persons are carried away into the institution, thus rendering the persons depleted. We are now in a position to see how these findings relate to, and answer, the problem we started with at the beginning of the book. I gave, in Chapters 1 and 2, quotations from Denis Martin and Tom Main showing just that kind of specific harm to the personalities of the patients caused by the institution itself. It was not just the illness they were there for, but the effects of being in the institution itself. The patient loses the active and overtly powerful side of themselves. So, we have now reached the initial goal of this book: to understand how these areas of identity were stripped away from patients in the old institutions.

Main showed how the helpful side of patients accumulated within the personalities of the staff. The helpful 'unconsciously *require* others to be helpless while the helpless will *require* others to be helpful' (Main 1975, p.61). Certain characteristics disappear from patients and accumulate in the identity of the staff. Personality characteristics were redistributed and relocated between patient and staff in processes based on the affect flow just described, to restructure the personality of the hospital. Eventual definite harm is done to those who need help in a care institution. And perhaps to the staff as well.[3] This is a plausible description of the occurrence in the old mental hospitals.

It is a description of unethical relations, a psychic corruption, an exploitation of the mind. The projective processes, re-ordering the personalities of those within an institution, give a profound dynamic meaning to the assertion that the person is 'the ensemble of social relations'. The therapeutic community is above all a self-conscious set of social relations, an institution that sets store by understanding them. If the therapeutic community has any influence on its members, it must do so in some deeply personal or internal way. And, above all other therapies, its influence is via the social relations.

The characteristic emphasis in the community is to support this healthy side of patients within the context of everyday life – the 'work of the day' (James 1987; Kennedy 1987). In this sense, the therapeutic community opposes the characteristic removal of the active side of patients, which has rendered them caricatures of helplessness. But it aims to do this with more than rhetoric. In Chapter 11 the practice of the therapeutic community emphasises responsible action, and sets up real work within a reflective context. Thus, the patient and the nurse work together in different roles. A patient is regarded as capable of carrying significant degrees of responsibility provided they get enough initial support and the nurse works 'alongside' to offer that support (Barnes et al. 1997). The work of the day is ordinary activity performed in the far from ordinary social relations of the therapeutic community. The pressure of support to carry responsibility is a direct, active (and largely non-verbal) reversal of the projective system that carries the personal life of vulnerable people away to become institutional energy.

Thus, the therapeutic community puts pressure on alienated people to internalise an active, responsible self again. This reverses the psychodynamics of alienation in the large mental hospitals and redistributes help once again, now in a more equitable direction. I claim that this system of support for responsibility at the level of action goes beyond the simple solutions of the kind I mentioned at the beginning of this book. It is not a blind surface change. It takes account of deep and internal processes.

In this sense I claim we can regard the therapeutic community as ethical in intent at this deeper level of psychodynamic exploitation. The early and charismatic pioneers who changed mental hospitals in the 1940s had some intuitive grasp of this need to tackle the endemic redistribution of responsibility and to introduce a dynamic restitution of it. An explicit formulation of this intuitive grasp has had to wait for the development of theoretical understanding of groups and institutions and the role of projective processes at these interpersonal levels.

The therapeutic community, in my examination, appears to offer an ethical alternative to the institutionalisation of the large mental hospital. In institutionalisation, projective processes appear to be allowed to run unchecked in a manner that would be unethical were it noticed – and since these processes, despite operating at an unconscious level, are now understood, it is unethical not to notice them. This has been the goal of our journey. I have tried, on the way through, to indicate many resources we have for dealing with these processes, especially in Chapters 9 and 11. These resources reside in the capacity for all to take thought; and for all of us to create reflective space in our groups and institutions.

But our journey is not quite complete. Whilst proceeding towards our goal of understanding institutions, psychiatry has moved on, the goalposts have changed position. We now contend with community care within society at large, which impacts explicitly on us and our practice.

Notes

1   To complete the description, there is a third 'state of mind', one suffered by Margaret, in which the disturbance is not contained at all, and her mind can be said to be neither in a state of comprehension nor of incomprehension. Instead there was a raw experiencing of bodily sensations, about which there was no curiosity.

2   Nick Manning (in a personal communication) suggested the term 'emoton', evoking a comparison with the particles of subatomic physics, like electrons.

3   I will not go into the harm to staff. It is to be found in terms of the stimulus to their omnipotent thinking and the ensuring demands of themselves that lead ultimately to the syndrome of 'burn-out'.

PART IV

The Alienated Commodity
and Market Psychology

Introduction to Part IV

The therapeutic community, like mental hospitals and psychiatry, exists within society at large. I shall develop, in Part IV, the importance of the surrounding society which impacts on and defines in many conscious, but also unconscious, ways the attitudes and beliefs within our communities. The themes which have emerged from the work concern the central importance of social relations as a defining context for subjective experience. Individuals experience their identity in relation to others, and that includes the unconscious relations which distort identity.

The chapters here start (Chapter 15) with certain assumptions which underlie psychiatry and the relations in our service with patients. The line of argument in this book calls a number of assumptions into question. And much rhetoric which often seems to be based on the way things naturally are needs to be recognised as socially generated and as varying over historical periods.

In Chapter 16 I attempt to create an understanding of the characteristic social relations in Western society based on choice, and how that bears on the dynamics we have found in the institutionalising process in mental health institutions. Blinded by implicit cultural attitudes, psychiatry is hindered from properly addressing these processes as they impact on the most vulnerable members of society. Although I quote Marx on alienation, which may be objectionable at the present time, the argument is less than Marxist in that it does not accept economic factors as the *only* determinant. Subjective experiencing has a part to play in setting natural limits to the effectiveness of economic pressures (Hinshelwood 1996a). The underlying processes that help to construct the sense of personal identity, and which I have described as formative in institutions, apply whatever political programme is in the ascendancy.

Finally Chapter 17 comes to the contemporary issues in community care as seen refracted through the social and institutional processes I have described. Those dynamics operate not only in our mental hospitals but more widely in society at large and they affect the community care currently provided by our psychiatric services. The role of therapeutic community principles in reflecting on these social influences is addressed.

CHAPTER 15

Alienation and its Assumptions

In Part I of this book, we discovered complex and hidden processes by which persons are formed and deformed in the institutions they inhabit. The last few chapters have dealt with the way those deformations can result in severe loss to the individuals but with a gain of 'energy' for the institution. This state of alienation of the individual has important consequences. We saw from the beginning that the repudiation of the active self of the inmates could function as an invitation to accept them as dependent and thus not responsible for themselves or others. But in this chapter, I want to describe briefly other implications, ones that should make us reconsider the assumptions we hold about human beings. I shall describe three areas where assumptions in psychiatry about the nature of human beings need to be reconsidered in the light of these unconscious processes: the notion of personal autonomy; the idea of a neutral scientific carer; and the essential quality of integration.

Assumption concerning autonomy

Treatments in psychiatry rely in part on a set of background assumptions, and so does the professional ethics of psychiatry, and in fact the ethics of all those practices which aim to influence people. The central aspect of the institutionalising process, which I have concentrated upon, is the loss of the active self, the part of the person that has initiative and can make decisions and take action on them. Contemporary parlance would describe this as the autonomy of the person. In psychiatry, persons so often lose their autonomy, and this is typically dramatised in a compulsory admission and the ensuing loss of ordinary civil rights. Although the right to appeal has been substituted for the lost civil rights, under 1983 legislation (in the UK), that substitution only confirms that the essential social discourse over schizophrenia is whether the patient can achieve autonomous functioning.

The ethics of psychiatry is, like that of medicine in general, based on the patient's capacity for personal autonomy, and the health worker's full respect for that. There is however a difficulty in psychiatry where the 'illness' is in the realm of abnormalities of autonomy itself. The topic has been debated by many people (Fulford 1989; Laing 1959; Szasz 1961), but despite an antipathy, it is generally accepted as ethical to over-ride a patient's autonomy when he is not capable of rational thought (Gillon 1986). There are however serious problems with these assumptions about autonomy (Hinshelwood 1997a and 1997b).

Autonomy is the central pillar of the right to make an informed consent about one's own treatment. If a person is deemed incapable of autonomy he must be approached on the basis that the health professional makes decisions for him. The shock of this position for patient and for society in general derives, partly, from the very great importance that autonomy plays in our view of the human being. To be incapable of making one's own decisions means one is either a child or a non-person.

However, personal autonomy has not always been such a central plank in the nature of the individual person. It is a view that has steadily grown over the period of modernity; that is, it originated in the late Middle Ages (Taylor 1989). There may have been fluctuations in the importance of personal autonomy, but that importance generally increased overall. One of the dips (i.e. dips in the importance of the individual in this respect) was in the period of World War Two, when the individual was mainly to be devoted to the cause of the community and nation of which he was part – that is, a cog in the war-machine. Interestingly the therapeutic community movement started in the communalism of this period (Hinshelwood 1989b), and has to a degree retained that sense of the person as being fully a person only when making some communal contribution of himself and his self-expression.

The communalism of the 1940s and 1950s changed abruptly when the permissive 1960s celebrated the individual; and then the emphasis in therapeutic communities swung towards permissiveness, and towards learning from a freedom of experiencing. I shall not continue here with the subsequent phase in which individualism was drawn into a monetarist philosophy from 1979 onwards, but will come back to that in the next chapter.

The trend towards increasing importance of personal autonomy means that a situation, such as in psychiatry, in which one person makes a decision for another is now highly contested. The pressures towards an unrestricted autonomy has contributed as much as anything to the general suspicion of expert knowledge which can surreptitiously manipulate and exploit the less knowledgeable. The protection of the individual is achieved by the requirement for informed content – that is, the expert, with his knowledge, is required to inform the patient of all the relevant facts of his condition, the alternative courses of action, and the probable outcomes, for the patient to make his own decision. However, my line of argument about the relations between patients and staff in psychiatry leads to serious problems for the notion of an informed consent. This is because the concept of informed consent is neglectful of anything but the conscious level.

What might a patient be consenting to at an *unconscious* level? Does he consent to the redistribution of his personality that is rife in psychiatric institutions? This is a difficult question to answer when we consider the kind of unconscious complicity described in Chapter 4. There appears to be an unconscious consent to an unconscious process. It is even more complex when we consider compulsory admissions, which under these circumstances may not be as compulsory as they appear! Consciously there is no consent, but unconsciously there is a complicity in relocating the active self in the staff. Processes of splitting and projection greatly confuse the issue of consent, which has unconscious as well as conscious aspects – aspects which may turn out to be in conflict with each other within the one person (Hinshelwood 1995, 1997a and b).

If the mind is to make autonomous decisions between alternatives, that person must hold both those alternatives in his own mind consciously. I claim that, in order for someone to make his own decisions, he needs to be integrated in his mind in this way – sufficiently integrated to be at war with himself. But in our case the patient's solution to his problem (losing the active side of himself and leaving it within the staff) depletes him of the power to make proper autonomous decisions. Ordinarily, in a *medical* practice the doctor would consider finishing the treatment if the patient is no longer consenting. But, in psychiatry and psychotherapy, the professional must do something different. The job is about precisely the means and mechanisms by which the patient disclaims his own choices. Instead of debating continuing treatment, the health professional continues treatment by working upon that alienation and depletion. He seeks a kind of meta-level of treatment – *treating precisely the problem of consent.*

Thus, the implications for our line of reasoning here is that consent cannot come before the notion of treatment, but is a quality dependent *on* treatment. And this renders consent severely problematic. Nor can we assume autonomy an inherent property of human nature. Such an assumption makes the practice of psychiatry more distinct from life and other professions than it really is.

Assumption concerning dislike

I want to turn to a related assumption. Psychiatry has taken upon itself the mantle of science, but has thereby created a further problem. The assumption is that the observational stance of the mental health worker is that of the natural scientist, objective and empirically verifiable. However, it is not so. Observation in psychiatry is complex since the observer must to a great extent employ a subjective awareness of his patient. And, moreover, what he observes is to a great extent the subjectivity of his object of study. In large measure the science of psychiatry is the engagement of one subjectivity with another. It is assumed that the advance of psychiatry is simply the reliable conversion of the features of those subjectivities into objectified and measurable scientific facts that will stand outside subjectivity.

But the problem is that subjectivity is uneliminable. Its traces hang around untidily. And this is itself observable. Elsewhere, I noted that two types of patients were characterised by the typical, subjective reactions they evoked in their carers – chronic schizophrenic patients, and severe personality disorders (Hinshelwood 1999b). I do not propose to describe this in detail; however it can be argued that the pressure within psychiatry to convert subjective observation to objective scientific facts, of the kind that a natural scientist deals in, renders the patient a passive, inert, even inanimate object of study. And what is more, my stress in this book has been that certain patients, chronic schizophrenic ones, are complicit in inviting being treated in this way. Thus, the very process of pushing towards a scientific psychiatry unwittingly plays out a schizophrenic's own method of coping – his loss of his active, decisive initiative.

This depersonalisation of the schizophrenic patient is in my view driven by the way mental health workers experience schizophrenic patients. It is a difficult experience which makes the staff remove themselves to an impersonal distance because of the discomfort which they dislike. For instance, the disagreeable experience of a chronic schizophrenic is reported in a letter by Freud:

> I did not like those patients... They make me angry and I find myself irritated to experience them so distant from myself and from all that is human. This is an astonishing intolerance which brands me a poor psychiatrist. (Freud, quoted in Haynal 1988, p.59)

It was a confession about psychotic patients. Freud suffered a disagreeable feeling. They were difficult for Freud because he couldn't relate to and understand them. And he wanted to. It is my contention that in the end the condition is one that frustrates and exhausts the enthusiasm of workers. Their experience of their patients becomes, swiftly enough, an assumption about their patients. The predominant assumption might be: such patients, without active initiative, are not fully human beings; we cannot relate to them.

These subjective experiences become assumptions about the nature of these persons, and then motivating forces in the life of our institutions. Although we can see that institutional dynamics enmesh patients in a process in which their active selves are continually carried away through the network of other people, the conscious assumption can grow up that it is their nature to lack the agency of a true person.

In order to observe their patients accurately and fully, psychiatric workers need to attend to this layer of subjective reacting. In other words, subjective observation cannot occur without the observers' reflection on their experience, in this case the subjective, psychodynamic states of the team. Sets of assumptions that underlie our practices need constant attention. I have called that attention 'reflection', and it is to be sustained by a culture of enquiry.

That assumption about the distance from which to observe schizophrenic patients needs questioning and reflection. But it can be specifically informative in the way that Heimann's (1950) classic paper made countertransference a source of subjective information. The staff reaction, to depersonalise their relations with their patients, can inform us of the processes which the schizophrenic person is, on his side, inviting. We ought now to make these assumptions the focus of attention in psychiatry itself, as the therapeutic community has pioneered with its culture of enquiry. In this case, we need to reflect on the retreat into an impersonal scientific mode of observation.

Assumption concerning integration

Someone who does not share the same world of meaning as oneself feels not quite human. Although there is wide public awareness of this problem in the confrontation between different races and cultures, in a smaller, and often more intense, way, this confrontation with meaninglessness occurs in the encounter of staff with psychotic patients.

Barratt (1996) did in fact proceed as recommended above and he made observations of the standard processes that occur in a psychiatric team dealing with schizophrenic patients. He concluded that there were four steps in a patient's typical course through the psychiatric unit. At first, the patient is perceived (and dealt with) as an object, one who does not live in the world of ordinary meanings. Then, second, he is dismantled into a set of symptoms and pathologies, that can be recorded objectively by neutral carers. This is followed by step three, a reconstruction of the patient as a 'worked-up' case, in which the patient's various 'objective' signs and symptoms are combined into a picture which is now meaningful, psychiatrically – he has a diagnosis, a set of treatment interventions and a prognosis for his future.

The second of these steps, the scientific process which dismembers a patient into parts, parallels, and is the counterpart of, the unconscious institutional process in which the patient comes apart and is dispersed in the institution's relational network. And step three reconstructs, and brings parts together – but in a mechanical, depersonalised fashion. It is a way of constructing a meaningful picture again out of the person, and is assumed to be a complete one because it does carry meaning. However, that assumption of integration is erroneous since some essential, active ingredient of the person is ignored. Integration has to be focused around his own agency in composing and holding himself together.

Barratt states that another piece of work must be done. Having become a worked-up case as an object of scientific study and record, the patient still needs to be reinvested with subjectivity as a person. This fourth step is interestingly described by Barratt as involving the reactions of the professionals; that is, their subjectivity. This final step requires the patient to be restored as an agent with volition – and his volition requires moral evaluation from us. Or, in other words, his subjectivity is confirmed by our moral and subjective evaluation of him. We like or dislike, we agree or disagree, etc. with him. We hold patients responsible for how they are and what they do. In other words there must be an engagement with the patient again in a world of meaningful intentions and actions. In this way the patient is returned to being a person, and rescued from the category of a 'case'.

The important point is that professionals normally avoid moral judgements about their patients, but in doing so they inevitably denude patients of a personhood. That professional requirement for a moral neutrality seems to be based, in the case of schizophrenia, on the assumption that the patient is to all intents and purposes a mechanical set of functions that is expressed in the recording of signs and symptoms.

The assumption is that the schizophrenic patient is sufficiently recognised as a set of parts. The attempt to restore those parts to a whole can only be partly successful – and it remains partial until a subjective reflection occurs based on personal reactions and evaluations. That subjective and non-neutral element of care in scientific psychiatry needs much more recognition. But that cannot occur till those assumptions about an integrated person are questioned.

Assumptions and reflections

I have picked out certain assumptions that underlie the psychiatric relation with patients. Patients are assumed to be certain kinds of objects (not persons). These assumptions determine the forms of psychiatric treatment and care. But being assumptions they are, like the air we breathe, essentially unobserved, and taken for granted. The value of the therapeutic community is that it prompts reflection on the cultural 'air we breathe', refuses to take human nature for granted, and provides possible alternative ways of thinking about the persons we encounter.

The therapeutic community is a treatment based in responsible action which can and is evaluated, and therefore it works against the alienation of mutual projective systems typical of mental health institutions (Hinshelwood 2000). It supports the general notion of the patient being a decisive human being. However, therapeutic community work often conflicts in this respect with general social assumptions. In some respects, the reflective capacity at the root of therapeutic community work is subversive of much more than psychiatry. In the instance of the assumption of autonomy, it questions an assumption about human beings that is widely held by society.

When there is not adequate reflection we have seen how there is a progressive distortion of the personalities of the members of an institution and a ritualisation of problem-solving. The professional accumulates health in himself, and the staff group. This is equivalent to a different kind of accumulation: the capital accumulation of wealth within one class. We, of course, are speaking of a kind of capital accumulation of health. In my view the problem of recovery is not easy to recognise precisely because the processes are so similar and linked to processes of exploitation and alienation in society at large. The social acceptance of such processes makes it more difficult to recognise and evaluate the malignity of them in the mental health field.

I shall turn to a further discussion of the assumptions underlying exploitative accumulation in the next chapter.

CHAPTER 16

Health Capital

In this chapter we will ask what the place of this psychological exploitation is in society at large, where the psychiatric service has to situate itself. Professionals are in a position to extract health, as it were, from their charges. This unconscious process is nevertheless an exploitation. Even though it is unconscious, it remains exploitation, and unethical.

Surplus value and depersonalisation

Alienating processes elsewhere in society reinforce those in the mental health service. The 'ensemble of social relations' tends to have an alienating quality in Western manufacture-based societies. Characteristically it derives from the industrial revolution. In industrial manufacture, the individual is alienated from himself, as he no longer has self-determination, or rather his self-determination has been reduced to a very slender minimum, the act of selling his labour, and that relation is equivalent to the reduction of the patient in a mental hospital, resigned and co-operative and too passive to cause any trouble, as Martin (1955) put it. The sale of his labour allows the employer then to remove from the labourer an aspect of his personal self – his creative work. That product concretises the psychological loss. The product of the creativity becomes the possession, no longer of the worker but of the employer who has bought the labourer's time, and removes the product into another realm, to become an abstract and impersonal thing. The employer converts the product into money and capital. Through the adroit manipulation of the exchange value (price) of the work product, and the labour costs, the work generates what is known as 'surplus value', i.e. profit which accumulates as an abstractable element of the exchange value after cost of production has been subtracted. Surplus value is a depersonalised, or reified, entity. It is depersonalised because it no longer belongs to those workers whose labour created it. It comes free of its moorings to exist as movable capital, an abstract form of value that leaves the producer depleted. This kind of view originated in Marx's[1] early writings.

> We shall start from a present-day economic fact. The worker becomes poorer the more wealth he produces, the more his production increases in power and extent... This fact simply means that the object that labour produces, its product, stands opposed to it as something alien, as a power independent of the producer. The product of labour is labour embodied and made material in an object...this realisation of labour appears as loss of reality for the worker, objectification as loss of and bondage to the object, and appropriation as estrangement, as alienation. (Marx 1844, pp.323–324)

This describes a process of considerable interest to our theme; the loss of some psychological part of the person which is drawn away from him in a very concrete way as the goods he produces but cannot feel identified with, in an exact parallel with the processes in institutions I have been describing (Hinshelwood 1983). Marx's later writings concentrated on how the worker loses in the competition for monetary wealth and thus he neglected that aspect of the early writings which concerns the worker's loss of his personal strength and identity.

Surplus value demands the reduction of personal work to impersonal capital. And thus, the work and the work product is a commodity just like the raw materials. Work and raw materials are alike to the accountant. The reduction of the labourer's work to a cost that is collateral to the raw materials depersonalises him to the level of a commodity, comparable to the raw materials. The result of this process is the characteristic distribution of wealth amongst owners and employers.

Although the actors in the roles of owner and labourer have modified in the 150 years since this kind of formulation was set down by Marx, the outline of what it describes has stayed more or less the same. The process results in an inequitable distribution of wealth, and a massive enhancement of capital accumulation. That concept of alienation in industrial institutions is remarkably similar to the processes that redistribute parts of the person in healthcare institutions. In the psychiatric service there grows up a similar inequitable distribution of health. And in both processes something psychological is separated off and moved through the institutional network, to accumulate in others who then seem – and, thanks to this process, actually become – more powerful, wealthy and healthy.

However, instead of pursuing that problem here, I shall concentrate on the observation that distribution of health in the course of health production appears to depend on a very similar psychological mechanism to that which occurs in the distribution of wealth in Western industrial production (Hinshelwood 1983).[2]

The developing healthcare system

The provision of care at the level of the individual meeting of patient with nurse is not necessarily impersonal, but the rhetoric of our institutions of healthcare, as they develop, depersonalises and treats health as a commodity to be produced by the institutions. Such intense personal contact as there is becomes, under the rhetoric, increasingly a commodity the institution possesses and can dispose of. Increasingly in our culture, healthcare is simple health production. Those side-effects for the person that arise from the unconscious psychological dynamics that I and others described (Foster and Roberts 1998; Obholzer and Roberts 1994) are ignored. In many Western countries financial accounting practices that were evolved for tracking wealth production have simply been adopted as the finance systems for health production. I suggest that such a change indicates an unthinking attitude towards activities in the non-industrial sector (care and service 'industries', as they are now called). Health (and service in general) are increasingly commodities which resemble raw materials, industrial products, and potentially abstract wealth. Health statistics too are a developing resource for the production process; and estimates of the nation's health are published in a way that suggests an abstract notion of health can exist in a reified form. It becomes a real, existing quality and quantity, somehow divorced, or split off, from the actual individuals who suffer good or bad health,[3] or those carers and patients who produce it.

Changing values

Over the historical period which this book reflects upon, since the 1940s, value itself has changed. During the latter half of this time, there has been the rise of monetarism – a logical extension of the idea of surplus value to wider and wider spheres of human activity. Values have become increasingly objectified, and that 'object' is money. This 'value of values' is a system used to 'put a price on its head' for all things. A particular movement has occurred, typical of the reason-based societies in which we now live. Money returns the abstract to the concrete; abstract value becomes material wealth: traditionally the material was physical – gold.[4] And in this process two things happen: first the abstract has become depersonalised, and reified ('thingified'); and second, its material nature, typically in the form of gold, makes it a 'natural' value, a sort of God-given value that exists in nature itself before and independently of people and society. The implicit argument is that what we have created socially – however iniquitous – is unavoidably natural. It is the naturalisation of social problems so that they cannot be addressed or rectified. In this way modern life has become more and more devoted to the objectification/reification of value itself.

Also, at the same time other values have faded.[5] In particular we revealingly call non-monetary values 'human values'. So, if caring for humans is to be valued it requires a price tag. It is then 'valued' as the price, and battles have to be waged to support the non-evaluated aspects of medicine – generally called, because any sophisticated terminology has been ignored, the 'quality of life'.

The rise of monetarist systems of evaluation has led to processes in society at large that are comparable to those in institutions in mental health. And I am moving now to include problems in institutions devoted to healthcare of all kinds, not just mental health. The problem is that money is not a simple value – as any other; it is a complex baggage of subsidiary values which are derived from it or which have simply stuck to it from past associations. In the case of healthcare, money implies the value of commerce, and commercial life is about survival.[6] The work is no longer directly about the survival of patients, but about the survival of the institution's commerce. Human values expressing the high value to be placed on human beings, *per se*, then have a re-entry problem in institutions such as healthcare ones. They are required to exist under the monetarist rule of the natural law of economics, accounting etc., as in some sense a subsidiary value to money. To do this health must be reconstructed as a value insofar as it can be shown accountable to audit, and the rules of accountancy. It is not a prime 'good' to look after other human beings. The prime 'good' becomes the demonstration – and comparison – of the monetary value of various forms of care.

This creates a powerful impact on ethics. The very success of industrial technology and production of material goods has not surprisingly led to adopting those systems in the provision of services. This has coincided, roughly, with changes in the way our society sets about capital accumulation. Whereas originally manufacturing created capital by supplying the demand, there has been an increasing emphasis on manipulating demand in order to maximise it and thus increase the need to supply, from which capital can then accumulate at a faster rate. The focus on supply has changed the way a worker is viewed. No longer merely a debit on the balance sheet of production, he re-emerges as a consumer whose demands can be supplied. Or rather, the worker would also have become a consumer if those aspects of the same person had not already been carried away in different directions, never to be reunited again, except in the most superficial recognition. This period, in the last half of the twentieth century, has been characterised in various ways, as late capitalist or postmodern. But these terms apply to a loosely collected set of characteristics which include the move from the emphasis on production to one on consumption, the rise of more and more efficient communications, particularly television and the internet, the emergence of society in general into a post-industrial age, where leisure has acquired a new and highly prioritised meaning, and a set of cultural schools generally termed 'postmodernist', which implies a style concentrated upon montage, pastiche and the favouring of surface over depth. In the view I offer here, it has also meant the radical push for new values, connected with the ability of money to quantify hitherto unquantifiable qualities, and the rise of management 'science' to serve that value change.

Choosing choice

The creation of consumers in the market, sometime in the first half of the twentieth century, has been a major way of increasing demand during the later decades. There are many economic complexities that arise from this rebirth of the worker as consumer, coinciding with the rise of self-conscious postmodernism (Featherstone 1990). I can only dwell on some aspects of this change.

Western culture has prioritised the individual, with an increasing preciousness, and prized his 'personal autonomy'. The rising emphasis on consumer demand has brought to the fore a rhetoric that now defines the individual in those terms. He is no longer a worker giving up his labour as an element of his personhood. Instead he is transformed, in the sealed-off segment of life called 'leisure', into a consumer. There his role is to make choices about the goods to buy and consume. However, the individual's role is now squeezed down to the function of making autonomous choices of what to consume. So, whereas once the worker was reduced simply to the function of selling his labour, now he is reduced to the function of consumer choice.

Choice is central as the motor for industry, manufacturing and services. So, the core value of consumerism remains autonomy – but it is an autonomy reduced to making choices of goods to purchase – and thus, above all, how to spend money. The capitalist hegemony over services has brought health production into line with wealth production and this has provoked a profound change in the social relations in healthcare, in the attitudes that they support and the values that become dominant. A health worker is now reduced, like his industrialised brother, to a depersonalised service professional. Reduced to a commodity, his efforts (labours) can then be exchanged as commodities, value given by the monetary exchange involved in his pay. Reduced in this way to a worker within a value system that prioritises the money exchange, he, and most notably his clients with him, will lose the 'human values' inherent in human beings; in other words, how can commodities 'care for' each other? Instead, choice – the freedom to choose one's purchase of material goods – invades healthcare as the freedom of choice of treatment; that is, informed consent.

Replacing human values

The power of consumption has put pressure on the service providers' part of the bargain.[7] The reliability of provision in the face of the power of the consumer's money has given rise to, amongst other things, 'risk-management'. Risk can now be quantified in an actuarial manner (Foster 1998a; Kemshall and Pritchard 1996), and can therefore be drawn into the monetarist value system. Reliability and quality is computed in terms of the risk of paying compensation, legal suits etc. The notion of risk-management – that is to say, the cost estimation of accidents and mistakes – is on the upswing, certainly within healthcare, where there is such a consciousness that if treatment fails, death ensues – or more significant, the risk of a legal suit ensues. Survival of those who are ill – i.e. the antithesis of the principle of the survival of the fittest – re-enters as the monetary cost in terms of insurance and legal damages of failing to keep patients alive.

It is not that it is easy to 'reduce' human values to monetary ones, but the hunt for methods of doing it is in full tide. The insurance 'industry' as well as the legal profession (more in other countries than the UK) are increasingly important instruments in monetarising human values – i.e. for assessing the value of caring for human beings as a monetary value. Provision has thus become concerned with monetary valuations – and not with any direct concern for the consumers/clients. Indeed the development of the monetarist value system specifically replaces that concerned relationship. This emphasis on the monetary consequences over the relational consequences has led to a further important development. This is the erosion of relation values, specifically that of trust. If the reliability of the other partner is seen in terms of the balance of their monetary advantage over disadvantage, then relational values such as trust decline in favour of legalised contracts, watchdog agencies, and, in effect, distrust.

In touching on these developments in the providers' values, it is ironic that they are a response to elevating the value of choice in the consumer/client. In other words this presupposes a 'relation' between the two, provider and purchaser. We cannot really get away from that human valuation of relationships which define each other,[8] even though the typical social relationship is increasingly defined in terms of distrust.

It is obvious that this bleak picture of the erosion of human values is overstated, as I am merely unfolding the picture we get from the new rhetoric. People themselves remain relational and human, valuing concern, involvement, trust and prizing each other merely as humans. The trouble that I am drawing attention to is the potential for rhetoric to engender false consciousness in our institutions. Just as the exaggerated redistribution between the helpers and the helpless is a false consciousness, so is the exaggerated emphasis on autonomous choice. The alienation of the first phase of capitalism has been supplanted. A once-depleted person has now had the hole in his identity filled in – by the identity of 'consumer'. Promoted as the (supposed) engine of market forces, choice is now fetishised as autonomous *choice in what he consumes*. In other words, the individual remains shrunk to a single activity.

Cast in the mould of this false consciousness, consent for treatment becomes confused. Choice is the value that monetarism offers for the ethics of professional practices. Simplistically, the only ethical requirement is that the person has made an autonomous informed choice. But a therapy based in the psychoanalytic setting, or in the group and therapeutic community settings, so visibly shows how a personality can be dismantled. No real ethical protection can come from an emphasis on the original consent to treatment (see Hinshelwood 1997a). As autonomous choice reveals itself to be a false consciousness, and by implication, so too does 'consent', care is reduced, in this false consciousness, to making a choice of alternative 'products'.

Responsibility and power

Responsible choice and action are complex and must be closely connected to the social context of relationships – including the relations of care. As this book has shown the social relations of responsibility are complex and involve interpersonal dynamics that are as much unconscious as conscious. Despite the accumulated knowledge of this, professional relations are still so often considered in simplistic terms. Because the power of expertise is seen as powerful and thus endangering the autonomy and choices of the consumer, it is bad power, without exceptions. So clients' and patients' personal autonomy and choice must be strengthened against the one-sided power of the professional. In truth such strengthening and support is important, as it can protect against the bad use of expertise. But we must question whether the rhetoric of choice in our society does really strengthen responsibility and choice, when it has arisen from the impetus for accumulation of capital, in a survival competition in the market place.

Power-relations are seen in terms of the erosion, subversion or suppression of autonomous choice, but if autonomous choice is a flawed concept, a false consciousness, so must the standard version of power-relations. Power-relations would seem to be constructed on the idea of an autonomous individual whose power is eroded because he is not allowed to exercise full autonomy. But a more fair notion of power would include the exercise of powerful interactions *between* people who are interchanging aspects of themselves, and can then be evaluated as good power or bad power on the basis of whether the intentions of these interactions are to create the separation of rich personality characteristics from poor ones (see Hinshelwood 1997a).

The interchanging process is important for displaying a profound contradiction in Western society. If the development of the consumer economic system depends on stimulating wants and then supplying them under the false consciousness of choice, then this suggests that the economic system is systematically unethical since it subverts the autonomous power to choose by substituting a stimulated demand instead.

Moreover, a consumer's choice is subverted, too, by the technology of psychology. The great achievement of psychology has been in advertising. This combines a need psychology – as exemplified by Freud: the human organism is innately a need-satisfying organism – with a subtle process of giving information, but in a way which actually influences, even determines, choices. Advertisers not only determine which 'product' will satisfy the need best, but indeed create the needs which will be satisfied by that product.[9] Thus, the rhetoric of autonomy and choice leads straight back into the same problem of who in effect makes the choices. Thanks to advertising they are, to a large degree, heteronomous choices.

This combination of forces – the rhetoric of choice plus advertising – in fact plays on an aspect of human beings that is not their autonomy. It plays on their ability to give up higher functions of the mind by projecting them into some authoritative other.

However, expertise has potentially a good use as well. But that 'good' is not necessarily in preserving a client's autonomous choice *per se*. Informing of efficiency and effectiveness is only a part of professional power and responsibility: the professional must still make his assessment of the unconscious processes – including the choice to give up power and choice. The measure of 'goodness' lies as much in the latter task of assessment as in the former of informing.

In fact, in terms of the thesis put forward in this chapter, the expertise of the psychodynamic specialist can go some way to subvert the social relations that have developed around the depersonalising late capitalist consumer monetarism. That does consist of work on the issues (personal and of course social) which subvert individual choice – but also those issues which are hidden by the rhetoric of choice itself. The psychodynamic revelations suggest that the therapeutic community, and psychoanalysis, can in this sense be a subversive practice. They directly reveal the dynamics which are hidden by the rhetoric. Psychoanalysis achieves a meta-level of work on the obstructions to consent (personal and social obstructions), and the therapeutic community engages directly with that active and responsible self which has so destructively been given up to those destructive forces.

Notes

1   Of course, introducing the very name of Marx risks making the reader dismiss my point in this chapter as superseded by history. However, I would ask for pause to re-consider – especially to consider the irony that despite Marx's early vehemence against alienation, the achievement of Stalinist alienation 100 years later was as ghastly as any. The paranoid form Stalinist economics took does not necessarily invalidate Marx's early writing on the psychology of institutions. And particularly we should reconsider these psychological writings when we discover a remarkable similarity in institutional process from a quite different starting point.

2   The similarity at the descriptive level is so close it suggests a deeper link between Marxist psychology and psychoanalysis. However, it appears that there is a radical contrast if we look beneath the surface, to underlying theories. Marxism attributes the

effect to the relations that are forced upon people by the characteristic technical mode of production. A psychoanalytic view of institutions, that I have been working out, attributes the effect to the reactions against major human anxiety and psychological distress: in brief, an economic versus a psychological explanation; or an individual versus a social origin to the phenomena. For those, like me, who regard the similarity of the phenomena as so similar that some unifying theory should still be sought, see Hinshelwood (1996a) for a more detailed discussion of how to reconcile the theoretical conflict.

3   Also this depersonalisation has occurred in the office side of industrial production, with a massive increase in the numbers of white-collar workers, selling their time and skills as commodities – and increasingly such work is now being taken over, or assisted, by impersonal machinery. The attempt to reduce personhood itself to machine-like activities, artificial intelligence research and neuroscience departments is another fascinating and related story.

4   Of course in the present we are advancing into a culture in which the material, natural stuff of money is being transported back into a non-material substance, known now as 'virtual', through the complexity of the electronic versions of money, which neither have any contact with real valuable material substances, nor with the values that were originally residing in human minds and relations.

5   The service industries more than anything are imbued with 'human values' – a term used in contrast to money values (humanism as opposed to monetarism). The ensnaring into the net of service industries has involved the reversion of various relational contracts towards a mechanical mode. In particular a central change is the abolition of trust. Instead, service personnel are trusted only so long as they are visible and can be checked. They operate in effect like a piece of machinery – an airliner that needs to be serviced for faults at regular repeated moments. See Bauman (1995) for a similar examination of the clash of values in the market system.

6   This is another naturalisation project, similar, and related, to the device used by Darwin and Herbert Spencer, to return market competition to the natural world as the 'survival of the fittest' species, or the survival of the 'fittest' society. By using a cultural analogy to conceptualise nature they could seemingly ratify culture as natural and unquestionable (Young 1985). Money, in its connection to the market place, is associated with the values of competition and of the extinction of the unfit. Healthcare is dedicated to the care of the unfit and their restoration to health. In this sense monetarism as a set of values – enhancing the value of the fit ones – creates a particular clash in those institutions dedicated to the care of the unfit, i.e. in healthcare institutions.

7   For a number of thoughtful accounts of the managerialism that has overtaken life in academia, see Strathern (2000).

8   The attempt to corral 'relationships' within a quantifiable and thus monetarist set of values means removing relations from being personal to render them legal entities.

9   Freud's theory of drives was that the human organism is provided at the outset with certain standard instincts. These are unusually 'plastic'; in other words the human being is particularly capable of changing the object which satisfies his needs – or providing himself with substitute satisfactions which seem to do the job as well as the original object. Advertisers have discovered this 'plasticity' to be highly useable.

CHAPTER 17

Future Visions
Towards Community Care

The therapeutic community arose from the revulsion against the degenerated life of the overpopulated nineteenth-century asylums. That revulsion also spawned a parallel movement – community psychiatry and community care (Busfield 1986). The aim was not to reform the institutions but to do without them. The institution would be the 'community'; and here, 'community' meant the neighbourhood where the patient lived (or had lived). Various experiments were conducted to preserve patients' social roots in their community. Then, during the 1950s, in the midst of that ongoing process of reaction, came the new psychiatric 'wonder drugs'. On the swell of optimism that the new drugs engendered, the then Minister of Health, Enoch Powell, in 1960, laid out a policy to close all large mental hospitals within ten years, i.e. by 1970. In the event, those closures were delayed by more than two decades. However, the revulsion against the old institutions, the optimism engendered by the new drugs, the promising experiments with new non-institutional services, the capacity of pharmaceutical company advertising to create a rhetoric about treatment, and the political eye on saving money for the public purse became an unstoppable bandwagon. And the project has been more or less completed today.

The vision was one thing; the reality of community nurses and psychiatrists adrift from their institutions is another. The optimism quickly became tinged with foreboding. But currently optimism survives in a guarded form – partly this is because the remaining inpatient care, now mostly in general hospitals, has seriously deteriorated into what sometimes seems terminal demoralisation, with intractable problems to fill vacant medical and nursing posts across the country. So, community care must seem a better option whatever it is like. There are a number of critiques of community care, mixed in their assessment of the achievement; e.g. the contributions to Leff (1997) and Foster and Roberts (1998), with a tendency towards more positive or more reserved evaluations, respectively. Given the very great difficulties in emptying the mental hospitals, it is easy enough to put a negative spin on the result in the community, whilst others can find it a positive achievement to have managed the process at all, given the scale of the task and the unpromising people who had to be moved.

But as the successor to the old psychiatric hospitals, how does community care face up to the issues raised by this book?[1] I made the point initially that the legacy of the old institutions should be a sophisticated learning about them that would enhance the possibility of more therapeutic institutions today and in the future. So, to what extent are the reflections on institutions relevant to care in the community?

Unfortunately, the old institutions are frequently regarded as irrelevant, superseded, misguided, and to be forgotten by all except historians. It is mostly assumed that the deleterious consequences were left behind with the institutions themselves, and the bad state of residential psychiatry today has no links with the problems of the old mental hospitals. However, psychiatric services are institutions wherever they are, and the impact of those with psychotic and other intractable disorders is likely to be the same, wherever care takes place, and whoever gives the care. Something of the old institutions must therefore be carried forward into the new units in community care. How are they dealt with there?

Scepticism has frequently been expressed, not least in the wry comment that the mythical and non-existent 'community' is as unmotivated to give support as are those vulnerable people to receive it. Indeed it is the very community that ejected their loved ones in the first place. And this makes community care a much broader task and one which involves not just the chemical suppression of symptoms, but the personal support for families, and trust-building in a renewed relationship. Attention to relationships has become much more pronounced in the best of community care; and the 'community' can in fact adapt to the returning patients, and has now accepted day centres and day hospitals, outpatient clinics and injection clinics, as well as sheltered housing and residential hostels. Even informal arrangements have grown up – like the corner newsagent store which becomes a hanging-out place, like the old hospital canteen. However, one of the problems, noted from early on, was the tendency for the new units – hostels, day centres, etc. – to acquire the same old bleak, lifeless quality of the long-stay wards of the old institutions (see for instance Morris 2000). They have been dubbed 'wards in the community'. The resemblance may be significant.

We have achieved five main areas of learning in the discussions in this book: inter-group projective systems; the interpenetration of individual and social structures and cultures; the culture of enquiry; support for responsibility and action; and impinging factors from the socio-political context. In concluding, I shall summarise some essential points I have covered and then indicate the relevance of this learning for the organisation of community care (Hinshelwood 1996b).

1. Inter-group projection

In the mental health service the defensiveness against the impact of psychosis takes the form, most usually, of projection, and it is at the level of group-organised projections, into other groups. What is projected is typically helplessness, inadequacy and incoherence (the equivalent of meaninglessness). And those projections are frequently made across the major boundary, that between staff and patients. If the problem in so much of psychiatry is how staff (and indeed patients) cope with feeling helpless and inadequate when faced with the intolerable, then one tempting solution is to identify other and often unknown groups of staff as the inadequate ones – and that is frequently other community care agencies.

One of the important conclusions in this book is that unsupported stress leads to 'pathology' of the institution; and a major element of these pathologies is the distortion of group identities, and of inter-group communications. This is rife in institutions, but also there is evidence of it in community care, too. The inter-group level in community care is the network of relations between the various agencies. The potential for splitting and conflicts between agencies is rife, and now well-known. The splits are evident when a patient passes between one agency and another – from, say, an in-patient unit to a day hospital, to a community psychiatric nurse working at home, and with a social worker or general practitioner liaising. There is immense potential for community care to pull apart at the seams – hence the rhetoric that employs the term 'seamless care' as a form of whistling in the dark. And we know the consequences for the patient, and for the public, are disastrous if the seams gape.

Whereas within an institution, groups live side by side with each other, in community care, various agencies are often geographically as well as emotionally distant. Face-to-face meeting is reduced to a level where there is great difficulty in testing the reality perception of each other. The kinds of communication problems illustrated by Cooper (see page 49) are at a high risk, and yet hardly appreciated. The occasional inter-agency meetings, or even awayday/stocktaking sessions, are often planned on the basis that simply meeting briefly will dismantle the obstacles in the relationship.

However, in addition to having to sustain feeling helpless and inadequate there is the exposure to feeling excluded. Foster (1998b) described the fragmenting process of community care in terms of the triangular problem of the excluded third (see Chapters 7 and 8). This can lead individuals clinging very powerfully to a specific community care team, where belonging can be strong but by excluding others who work in other units/teams. This then provides a set of separated agencies and each can use another as the receptacle for the further projection of inadequacy, or exclusion – into 'them', and not 'us'. It is always possible, in community care, to identify some other agency to fulfil the role of the excluded one. In all the projective psychodynamics the professional anxieties which drive those barriers remain unaddressed.

There are a myriad of potential fault-lines in community care that can offer opportunity for the powerful forces to create barriers. The challenge is how to address these divisive processes, when the service is not all within the same walls of one institution. Foster's recommendation is to sustain specific attention to the three components of community care: mental illness, the carers (paid and unpaid) and the community.

These are complex inter-group dynamics. They are unconscious and produce uncontrolled effects on the working of the service. I will now turn to a systematic description of these phenomena in a community care service.[2]

Demoralisation: If many staff are subject to feeling despair, then the first danger to the team is that it will become collectively demoralised. Collective despair is a demoralised atmosphere in the whole team. People cannot give each other the support, encouragement and praise which is needed, when they themselves feel they are not doing a good job. There are many indices of demoralisation; some as simple as high rates of sick-leave, absenteeism and turnover of persons in the team. When all those things make the team feel unstable, members become mutually unsupportive. The morale tends to get worse. A disastrous spiral, or vicious circle, takes place.

Stereotyped patients: However, there are ways in which the team members can collectively help themselves. One is to deny the feelings of helplessness and despair and it is very common for them to agree that those feelings are located in their patients – only. A rigid perception of themselves and their patients grows up, as Main described in the quote at the beginning of Chapter 3 (page 45).

Scapegoating: Sometimes it can be limited to one patient who is elected into a position to carry all the hopelessness. He is 'scapegoated'. And he usually gets worse clinically – thus confirming the way the staff have decided to see him.

Routine: The meaninglessness of the patient's experiences and anxiety is very corrosive of the staff's ability to continue with sympathy and understanding. The distance to which the staff retreat can then be institutionalised by a systematic process of turning the work into a set of routines – one could say mindless routines.

'Paranoia': Alternatively the staff team can collectively change their direction of interest. Instead of feeling hopeless about their patients, a new attitude grows up. This is a view that the patients could be helped but there are not enough resources in the team. The problem is believed to be the authorities or managers who keep them so short of staff, of training, of money and so on. They feel together amongst themselves, as if under siege against their employers who don't understand them, or who are stupid, or who may be deliberately malign. The team can feel happy together, and maybe happy even with their patients, so long as they have an external enemy they can fight elsewhere.

Fragmentation: Or, alternatively, the team may become divided within itself. If each person has the feeling, absorbed from the patients, of being hopeless, then they can export that feeling by electing others *in* the team as the hopeless ones. This can lead to mutual denigration of each other, often not expressed. So nobody can really get a proper picture of who is doing good work and who is not. Realistic perceptions and mutual support are both lost.

Unco-ordinated agencies: In a similar process, one agency can project the despair and hopelessness into another team within the community services. Different teams therefore get into mutual denigration of each other – the domiciliary team, the day hospital, the in-patient ward, etc. Then the service itself becomes fragmented.

These various phenomena, occurring at the level of the organisation, impact back on the quality of the service. Inevitably it must get worse if these processes become established. Changing staff, high levels of absence and temporary staff, scapegoating of patients or other staff, and splits within and between teams must all have a very bad effect on the work done. In turn this will affect people's morale as they realise that they do not give the best chances to their patients. Under these conditions, job satisfaction reduces, and a descending spiral can set in.

2. Individual and social structure

The effect of the structure of the community upon a patient's ability to contain his own impulses, and to lock onto the community in a more thoughtful way, is very important. A service often on the edge of schisms, meets and takes in persons who are collapsing in fragmentation. There is a potential here for unrecognised mutual harm. In Chapter 8 we explored this interaction between intrapsychic and social structure, to discover the various forms of identification. When the individual identifies by equation, there is a profound joining of his fate to the service. This appeared in the illustration of 'A' in the day hospital (page 88)

A day hospital might be taken as a useful paradigm of the specific difficulties in providing coherent structure in community care. It has special characteristics in this respect. It exists in reality only from time to time – during the day, each day. Every morning the members, by arriving in the building, build the day hospital again. Their presence is essential for it to be, and therefore their arrival is an act of forming the day hospital structure. Everybody is involved in a more-or-less voluntary exercise of recreation. The community forming each day entails re-establishing the links between the individuals, and needs us to pay attention to what kind of links are being established today. We are driven to study the impact on the individual as the institution's structure varies. Every day the day hospital comes apart; and it reforms again the next day. For distinctly fragmented personalities this coming apart and reforming matches to a greater or lesser extent the fate of the minds of so many attending the hospital. And these minds may unfortunately move to its rhythms.

The individual has power. He can experiment with it by lateness or absence. His power over the community is much more publically declared than that of the in-patient. For some patients this power is greater than others. Their presence is more noticed in a community than others', and therefore their absence is more noted. For some this power is a great revelation and an exciting form of game to play. For others they feel a great responsibility towards their colleagues; sometimes crushed by the weight of this responsibility and guilt.

The culture of the day hospital will develop to deal with the turmoil of responsibility and guilt, or with the feeling of being played with. Attitudes arise to deny these anxieties – for example the attitude that individuals are free to attend whenever they want; that it does not in fact affect anybody else at all. That attitude is a lie, it reaches a peak in extreme forms of individualism. Other attitudes of coercive discipline may develop so that rules and punishments turn the anxiety into action upon each other.

Leaving the community at the end of the day entails separating and negotiating the particular problems of that potential sense of exclusion that was described in Chapter 7. We need to pay attention to what kind of result comes out of that negotiation; benefit will come from the ability to form an internal link with a 'community in the mind'. At the end of the day, the day hospital disappears, and evaporates into all the individual droplets of people that once made it up. This dissolution can eat deep into the heart of everyone as a corroding sense of entropy. The world of one's self during the day runs down – and dies. Everyone whose identity has bonded with the community feels equally fragmented. Each of us dissolves as the community dissolves. For those who are involved in an 'identification by equation', this can be a disaster, and needs special provision and support.

For many disturbed people in community care, fragmentation is a lifelong terror, the dissolution of their own being. The intermittent nature of the day hospital and other community care services recapitulates that fragile experience of existence – that they are themselves intermittent and easily disappear existentially. For others it is the final proof of their guilt, and a failure to support the integrity of the hospital.

The crucial moments for the day hospital, its forming and dispersal, are equally crucial for the minds of the members as well. Each of the two moments are fraught with turmoil about the institution's coherence experienced in the earliest emotions of the parental institution; that parental couple comes together, exclusively, or otherwise, and may be torn apart too. Such phantasies in the minds of the members are experienced in the daily fate of the day hospital, and members insert themselves, or otherwise, into that phantasy institution which they see played out before them. I have dwelt on the rhythm of the day hospital because of the origins of my own therapeutic community experience. But it connects with so many non-residential community care units which also close intermittently.

Those patients who form that unthinking identification have a problem with thinking, reflecting and knowing themselves properly. It needs the units themselves to sustain reflection; the staff in effect remain guardians of the function which can so abandon patients.

3. Culture of enquiry, sustaining reflection

Mental health needs to recognise itself in general as a reflective practice, a practice which expresses, in words or in actions, the thoughtfulness that has gone into it. A space needs to be opened for reflection, enquiry and linking to happen *between* people. Though this 'reflective space' might be based on psychotherapy, it is both more and less than psychotherapy. In psychotherapy, a reflective space tends to have the following four elements:

1. enquiry into repeated patterns

2. a respect for reality as it is

3. a supportive and non-judgemental system

4. a linking-up between those people who are engaged in the reflection.

The practice of psychiatry is less, in the sense that it is on the whole less thoughtful about the relations of care. But it is more, in the sense that psychotherapy does not have the answer to all the problems of sustaining reflection in our services and institutions. That is why the therapeutic community, concerned as it is with the maintenance of social institutions, has a particular part to play in investigating the problems of psychiatry as a whole. It is not of course that psychiatric institutions in general should ape the methods that therapeutic communities have specifically developed to deal particularly with severe personality disorders, over 50 years. But therapeutic communities have certain generalisable principles:

*   enquiry into ritual activities

*   respect for reality of relationships in the community

*   supportive but reflective systems

- maintenance of a healthy staff–patient relationship.

This knowledge, and practice, learned *within* institutions, can be transferred outside, to the care in the wider community. The important elements of the thinking are the notion of 'enquiring', and of the 'reflective space' in which to practise it. Community care often fails in both respects, and is in danger of acquiring a resemblance to the problems of its patients. The dispersed and often emotionally fragmented state of community care implies a seriously deficient container and lack of a coherent space for the separate parts to link together.

Unfortunately political pressure inadvertently works against the need for reflection: the Care Programme Approach (CPA), clinical governance, evidence-based practice and the general notion of 'best practice' can be reinterpreted in a way that inevitably tends to reduce the work to bureaucratic formulae. That is an anathema to real learning in the practice of human relations (see page 109). It is an escape from thinking and a reversion to blind practice – following the rules and rituals of forebears. It avoids the real struggles and uncertainties of problem-solving now. In the therapeutic community, these problems of containment, and the 'freedom from thought', are well understood. The real challenge is to find the appropriate kind of reflective space for community care. For instance, the CPA often dismantles patients into sets of parts, each cared for by a separate community care team; could the CPA instead be used for keeping lively links going between those agencies? Could clinical governance be rewritten to include an emphasis on problem-solving, and the enquiry into ritual practice?

The therapeutic community reflective space, though not necessarily a verbal one, places an emphasis on words in the community meetings and any small group therapy that is in the programme. In therapeutic communities, enquiry into ritualising problem-solving, the respect for reality, the non-judgemental support, and the relational links through the work of the day are frequently conducted through both verbal and active modes. But it is not in fact necessary to sit in groups with each other; and, in community care, not practicable either. Nevertheless, productive communication is necessary across barriers. Should we be exploring the uses of the new communication technology to help us here? A specific kind of virtual communication for dispersed communities may be available. These are innovations yet to be. And special understanding which the therapeutic community movement has amassed could help to pioneer them. Across agencies, the emphasis might be placed on continually invigorating each other's problem-solving, and stressing to each other the relational base of care.

Fragmentation, despair and meaninglessness are the crucial problems in the lives of patients and clients who we seek to help. It makes sense that they should find themselves in a service which is familiar with, and knows how to struggle with, those states. We expect patients to learn the struggle. The therapeutic community struggle is repeated in all the different care settings – large hospitals, small in-patient units, inter-agency work in community care, and informal family and neighbourhood support.

4. Support

Nurses and psychiatrists have been set adrift from their institutions in the community, and in search of 'rehabilitated' patients who are equally rootless. For all its rigidity, and the tendency to a therapeutic resignation, those old institutions had a stability, predictableness, and a place and role for all its members, staff and patient alike. Despite the distorting quality of those roles, there was no problem in feeling a belonging, and, though constricted, an identity. Back in the 'community', belonging is very fragile, and may be non-existent, and a proper sense of identity can easily fade in the anonymity of urban surroundings where most community care is located – to be replaced by disadvantageous forms of identity by equation. Belonging and identity, however corrupting in the institution, have been exchanged for the risk of a drifting anonymity or clinging identification in community care.

It is not just the patients who have lost this basic kind of support. It is also the community care workers, bearing the brunt of the difficult job, often face-to-face with their clients on the doorstep. This is very different from the comradeship (and sense of safety) of the nursing station on the ward, and the ordered hospital team. So, I am suggesting that without the large institution and its ordered team, the mental health professional often feels as much at sea as the discharged patient. The colleagueship of a team of nurses on the ward, a multidisciplinary team in the hospital, or a group of professions defined within a single institution, has been eroded. So, a colleagueship in the face of the trenchant impact of psychosis has proved harder to achieve in community care than expected.

But why is support so very necessary? We addressed early on the common distress that affects the workers in mental health (Chapter 2). Central to this occupational distress is the nature of psychosis. That impacts on staff, on the patients and on each other. The fear of madness is a ubiquitous anxiety – probably akin to the fear of death, and mental health workers are no less vulnerable than anyone else. The impact of psychosis is typically a direct one – that is to say, it is not mediated by words. It is the direct impact of the suffering visited upon others – like a mother apprehending the distress of her baby (long before the baby can communicate anything in words). Relationships, of course, are based on so much more than words. In fact, non-verbal forms of communication are now familiar. They are on the whole 'readable', that is they have a meaning. With psychotic patients one of the most difficult elements of the distress is a quality of meaninglessness. It seems to be the property of humanity to give meaning to their experiences, and psychotic patients, especially schizophrenics, fail at that. Members of staff are therefore confronted with that seeming loss of humanity in those they care for.

This state of fragmentation is accompanied as often as not by two other painful states – excessive responsibility (and guilt), and the sense of exclusion.

Responsibility often crushes. And staff are prone to that despairing sense of responsibility and failure, by the needs of the patients to express it – evacuate or communicate it. In the therapeutic community it was found to be important that a specific focus on responsibility, and on the necessary support to place it in a realistic context, became central, in the form of meaningful work. Responsible action engaged in jointly is the cornerstone of therapeutic community practice – more so even than verbal insight. In community care, responsibility is located by government directive – it is the key worker, or Care Co-ordinator, who must carry responsibility. However, no directive concerns the need for support for this task, and the need to achieve a realistic perspective on the felt responsibility and guilt. Community care therefore has a very clear focus for the place support is needed, and could, learning from the experience of therapeutic communities, be specific about the focus, nature and intensity of necessary support.

In community care the opportunity to feel helpless in the face of the suffering and meaninglessness is no less than in the old hospitals. But often with so much time working alone, the support is less and the responsibility is a greater burden carried in lonely fashion. The powerful means of support in the old institutions, of belonging to the working enterprise, is lost, and however degrading that may have been, the pernicious feeling of exclusion (Chapter 7) can arise without it. Being in an institution can lead most easily to a formal identification with it by equation. But if no coherent institution exists, then that recourse is missing and leaves the person potentially swept by feelings of exclusion. In the ensuing desperation, something else can happen – an identification with the incoherence of community care. And that threatens personal stability.

5. The social/political context

In our contemporary culture, working with people is politically and socially reduced to valuing commodities – lives, treatments, carers. This is not a condition for socially supporting mental health services. It enhances, too, the reduction of practice to depersonalised procedures or rituals. Thinking in commodity terms inevitably reduces the comprehension of the work by the paymasters and the bureaucracy who attempt to give the necessary support. And equally, the issues that arise in public opinion and the media are also inevitably dealt with in uncomprehending and unsupportive ways.

Against this tide in our culture, the mental health service has to try to sustain an island of counter-culture. Human values – the importance of relationships, the recognition of difficulties in human living, personal support and colleagueship, the need for help at all levels, and the place for emotional honesty – must survive against the onslaught of monetarist values. This is a predicament for all healthcare where the culture of care is opposed to the more ruthless business culture of the market, and where the survival of the fittest dominates as a principle. But it is especially poignant in mental health because the issues which patients bring are so extremely focused around the problems of human values.

Care in the community must, by definition, depend on a relationship. The very content of community care is, precisely, relationships; those between the client and the individuals who make up the community, family, neighbours and local organisations and groups. Insofar as community care has to be about relationships, it unexpectedly subverts the assumptions about psychiatric treatments based on a commodity choice of treatment – the right drug for the symptom. Relationships have been brought back into psychiatry in an insistent way in practice – whilst the rhetoric and false consciousness of commodity thinking excludes the idea of an individual being formed and sustained in his 'ensemble of social relations'.

Despite the false consciousness, in fact practitioners are aware of the relational nature of their work. The problem is that relations inevitably bring the emotional impact of the work, and a consciousness that excludes relationships excludes the possibility of real support for the impact on staff. Or alternatively, under the pressures to perform according to the rhetoric, they must ignore their own knowledge of the importance of the relational aspect of the work, and they sense the worth of their work is consequently undermined. Instead of relational work, they are thrown back to performance according to rules and guidelines of 'best practice'. They can relate to a 'manual' rather than a person. And thus the heart is taken out of the work – leaving them less distressed, perhaps, but devoid of job satisfaction.

The therapeutic community – RIP?

Much has been made over the years of the demise of therapeutic communities. It is all exaggerated. But it is an intensely context-dependent form of practice – dependent on the cultural context; and surviving only as it adapts and keeps its innovation within tolerated bounds (Hinshelwood 1989b). And so, as our world changes – our climate of social opinions, as well as fashions in psychiatry – the therapeutic community is always going out of date. It is always having to re-invent itself. But that is exactly the therapeutic communities' innovative project – to reinvent itself in a process of continuing innovation (Manning 1989; Punch 1974). Its relations with current monetarism, with the post-war period of reconstruction, with the 1960s' permissive individualism, have all been different and required both accommodation to prevailing values and a mild subversion of them.

In a sense, nevertheless, the therapeutic community is no longer an innocent and exciting new movement. It has grown up. It has new work to do. We need to be known as having understood something about those old institutions, of having learned something about moving an anti-therapeutic process towards a therapeutic one. Of having a tradition, an experience, to pass on. It is a tradition forged in change, and about the mechanism of sustaining life in new projects. There is a vision to be passed on for the future of psychiatry, and of living in the world. We can claim to be poised for a similar contribution to the difficulties in community care. Community care, a sister development of the therapeutic communities, properly conceived and practised, must share that quiet subversiveness.

Notes

1   See for instance Nathan (1998), drawing on Menzies (1988a); also Barnes (2000).

2   See Hinshelwood (1999a) for an extended treatment of these descriptions.

Epilogue
Living Together

This book has been a review of my experiences in therapeutic communities stimulated by an impulse towards liberation which was most clearly articulated for me by David Kennard. He wrote about the 'therapeutic community impulse' as a constant impulse to regenerate freer and less institutionalised organisations, an impulse that popped up in all sorts of walks of life. It is pleasing therefore to close this book with an epilogue that is a chapter I wrote (Hinshelwood 1996c) for a book David edited on the gifts that psychotherapy might make towards conceiving the 'good life'.

I Have an Idea...

> I cannot perch upon that rim of sky
> to search my world of corn and sand
> on which my feet now stand.
>
> *'The Horizon's Lure', unknown poet*

Introduction

Someone said, 'Beware of a politician with an idea.' But a politician needs more than an idea, he needs a group of supporters and voters to get the idea too. It needs to proliferate through a crowd. It is a bit like the flu. And yet having an idea is not felt to be a disease. On the contrary, it gives the exhilaration of conviction, a climactic sense of having a 'truth'. An idea has a natural progress from the mind of an individual, to become the core of a group. Otherwise it dies. With its promotion to a single-minded consuming passion, for its group of holders the entire world falls into place around the selected idea. Conflicts and other bits of misplaced litter in life become easily dealt with by the guiding principle of the idea. This pattern – the idea with its surrounding followers and its political consequences – is, loosely, what we call an 'ideology'. The creation of ideology appears to be a bedrock of life in a group.

We tend, instinctively, to suspect ideology, and for good reason.

I agreed to make a contribution to this collection of essays (Kennard and Small 1996) on the condition that it was not going to be a passion-piece about how psychoanalysis can come up with the idea that will make our society different, cure its sins, a new ideology looking for its gathering of supporters. I would like this piece to be a calm reflection; to be *about* politics though not *of* it. That cannot be. I cannot be outside of political debate.

The problem of 'position' is central to the theme of this essay. There is nowhere outside the global culture from where we can view the problem and its solutions, and no one in that nowhere. Yet there is always a queue of people claiming to be in that objective position. Indeed I argue that one of the prime causes of our difficulties is that so much of politics is done as if someone was looking in from outside.

In this essay I want to explore what a non-objective approach might look like; that is to say, a return to a politics looked at from *the inside*. But a return that has been marked by a new understanding of human beings. This exploration will entail quite a speedy traverse across a number of problems that people set themselves by aggregating together in societies. These include the problematic entanglement of passions with ideas that creates ideology; the mistaken solutions of pluralism on the one hand and of neutral fence-sitting on the other; and the quest for a different balance between these two – emotions and reason – in our political life.

Culturally we separate out, like oil and water, our emotions from reason. Emotions are recognisably of a moment and of a place; while reason claims a lofty independence and universality. Emotions are of a person, reason has a generality. Because of such polarities, they become each other's worst enemy. Animals have passions, and computers reason. We need a blend. Or rather we need a new blend, not the old impassioned ideas claiming reasonableness while driven by unacknowledged emotions. The quest for a different balance between emotions and reason must, I claim, be our new politics.

The problem

Our start must be this most dangerous period in human history, our generation's half-century poised for mutual nuclear destruction. It has been based in the ideas of Russian Communism versus the crusading Capitalist idealism of the West. Indeed, the twentieth century has been especially prone to economic ideas and ideologies. From the Stalinist degradation of Communism to the Fascism of Hitler and Japan, to the multitude of nationalist conflagrations which recently have seen spitefully inhuman attitudes destroy people in the Falklands, in Kuwait and the Gulf, and in Bosnia, as well as in so many impoverished Third World countries, we have been captured by ideas more than at any time since medieval theology tyrannised the post-Roman Europe. Ideas are the enemies of humans, so it would seem, despite the hunger we have for their poison.

Collecting together

Why is the Western world degenerating into a high-tech version of the squabbling city-states of ancient Greece? Have no lessons been learned? Probably it is not so simple. It is more than just the cussedness of individual human beings with a good idea in their heads which they can't let go of. It is in our rapidly expanding collectives that new problems of co-operation are encountered. The advance of technology, especially transport and communications, has brought together ever larger collectives of individual human beings. The ever wider net of communications, and the ever faster response times, ensure that ever larger numbers of people are drawn under the spell of good ideas. And this occurs at the very same time as larger numbers of people need to be drawn into co-operation with each other, rather than conflict.

Whether or not there is something inherently destructive in the individual human being from the beginning, there is something which is inherently destructive in human society. We must go to the human collective to understand these phenomena. Nietzsche asserted: 'Insanity in individuals is something rare: in nations, parties and epochs it is the rule.' And we are familiar with the fact that individuals may be good losers, but groups almost never are. The splitting of collectives of human beings into sects, factions, parties, classes, nations and blocs is different from the psychology of the individual human.

What therefore happens in a collection of humans, when it becomes possessed of an idea? A kind of identity takes them over. People can be consumed by the idea of their group, and in the end become its vehicles for expression. Cults can proceed to the actual bodily destruction of the people that make it up – from the mass suicide at Masada in the first century, to the suicide pilots of Japan in 1945, to the Branch Davidian sect at Waco, Texas, in 1993. This state of mind is seemingly mad in an individual, but within the group it is accepted as a sensible consequence. The most pernicious of all belief systems, that grows up with extreme speed, is the belief that 'my' group is good, 'yours' is bad.

People are like that.

Whatever a person is confronted with and reacts to is evaluated within a passionate good/bad dimension. And we evaluate, and are evaluated, all the time in the context of our social group. Indifferent ideas simply drop out of social existence.

It is a major transition to move from individual psychology to social psychology. The individual can hold an idea in his head without it necessarily taking a hold upon him with orgasmic fervour (though sometimes it does so). In the collective, it is almost as if there cannot be a collective that is not bound together by its idea. This especially seems so if such a collective can find another collective with a different idea – then, in a flash, 'different' becomes 'opposite'.

In fact we could go further and suggest that ideas and knowledge are social – are group behaviour. They are not just objects that an individual possesses. That is to say, ideas cannot normally be aroused to a level of conviction without the presence of someone else to confirm them. Anyone who has an idea on their own is regarded as having a bee in their bonnet, and being at least part barmy. Not so with a group of followers.

When a person comes up with an idea, he turns to others to confirm or disconfirm it. Some people are adept at getting wide agreement for the ideas they have. To some extent this is a matter of character, but also it is a matter of the social climate of opinions and of values into which his idea falls. So, it is in that context that a person has to evaluate, and in which he must form his beliefs. He must, because that is being a person. In another context that same person will have different beliefs. He has the chance of recognising something defective in his ideas. But until he changes that cultural position he is likely to be blinkered to real criticism.

False consciousness

Ideology is the false assertion that an 'idea' is universally true. It falsifies the consciousness of other truths – the truths of other ideas. The triumphant claims for the success of market forces have been proclaimed, and partially accepted in the last decade. They have swept forward without acknowledgement that there is another 'truth': the truth that people in our society need nurture from each other, not merely bracing competition. The ideology of market forces may have *some* truth in it (about regulating people's possessiveness), but it is a partial truth. It leaves out a truth that others know (perhaps known by those with fewer possessions). Together such partial truths might create a fuller truth; apart, they drive the heady passions of group allegiances.

A false consciousness believes that it can be objective when in fact we can only see from within our own position. It leads us to judge other people's beliefs in terms of the groups we belong to. We judge their values and ideas without belonging to them and without sitting in their position. This is the false consciousness of the bourgeoisie: that it can speak, objectively, for everyone. It is also the false consciousness of a proletariat. A class consciousness is not only a partial view of the matter as a whole, it is also an indulgence in a belief that it is not a partial view; and the pretence that we can speak for everyone by taking a view from outside.

And, when the idea does spread, ideology blindfolds the awareness of why it has done so. When Christianity spread across the globe in the nineteenth century, it was not noticed that the spread resulted from military and economic conquest, not from the power of good argument, faith or the power of love. In fact such conquest resulted from superior technology which itself arose out of the de-christianising influence of the Enlightenment. So, ironically, Christianity's success rested on non-Christian achievements. And was not noticed to do so.

Two people, in two different contexts, can evaluate and believe, not just differently, but in opposition. Then they can clash. Each will think the other is making a mistake; often attributed to malign motives in the other. Such is passion. Freud recognised this common occurrence within intergroup relations:

> ...it is precisely communities with adjoining territories, and related to each other in other ways as well, who are engaged in constant feuds and in ridiculing each other – like the Spaniards and the Portuguese, for instance, the North Germans and the South Germans, the English and the Scotch. I gave this phenomenon the name of 'the narcissism of Minor differences', a name which does not do much to explain it... [But by these means] cohesion between members of [each] community is made easier. (Freud 1930, p.114)

Inside the group it is difficult to recognise that relativity. Insight is lost. Ideas are constructs of suitable locations and these are group locations. A member of a Christian church will evaluate the missions in Africa in one way; those from an Enlightenment, humanistic background, in another way. The French evaluate the fortunes of Germany in passionate terms based on the national rivalries, rather than the self-interest implicit in getting along together. The problem is not that anything goes, but that different things go, in different places, and at different times. And those differences are very specific.

Such is ideology, the falseness of our consciousness. It is a collective kind of madness, an obsession/compulsion at the crowd level.

An example of the impassioned idea

One example of this 'mistaken' assumption of good reasons is the issue of aggressive begging. This has now come up more than once in our political debates in the mid-1990s, and not with just one political party. For perhaps good reason, politicians of all shades think it is a vote-catcher.

The issue came up in its own distorted way, but was an attempt to address the reaction we might have to these dehumanised persons – the beggars. To characterise the campaign: these ne'er-do-wells who take no responsibility for themselves and their physical needs, such as housing, food or gainful career, lurk in our streets; they are verbally and occasionally physically aggressive to passers-by from whom they demand the wherewithal to live which they are unwilling to find for themselves. It is possible to think of these people as simply deprived materially – hungry, cold and in ill-health. But it is more. And I think the reaction of people passing in the street is a profound anguish about the fate of a *person*. It is the fateful colleagueship with that degraded human being as well as the sympathy for their hunger which sparks a reaction in the well-fed passer-by. It is as much the destroyed person as the damaged body and its health. It is, however, that reaction to the person which is so much more difficult for us, who are more fortunate – and partly so because it is so much less articulated in our society. That was the picture presented, immediately taken up by the press, and clearly listened to with alarm and moral tutting by many normally well-meaning and charitable people. What was it that this campaign against these destroyed persons touched off in us?

As psychotherapists we know that it is very likely that what was struck was something not consciously known, yet readily active within the hearts of many people. First, most people, perhaps everyone, feels responsibility, and actually guilt, for suffering others. And the re-emergence of beggars so publicly in the last few years must have given rise to such feelings as these.

What begging does, therefore, is directly to assault us in our more humane feelings. This allows a deft sleight of hand in the aggressive begging campaign: the suggestion that the pain of sighting beggars could be a deliberate intention on their (the beggars') part; and therefore, being so ill-intentioned, they are ruled as unworthy of feelings of guilt or charity on our part.

Those feelings of ours – guilt and responsibility – are then rendered obsolete and they must go, as it were, underground (the psychotherapist understands that this is the function of the unconscious). Feelings of guilt then resurface elsewhere – in the beggars themselves. They are responsible for causing hurt and pain to us!

Of course it is possible, with matching outrage, to counter this picture by appeal to sympathy for the vastly greater number of extremely docile, harmless and defeated beggars who exist, in reality, on our streets; or to deplore the devastating meanness of the programmes of welfare cuts which have brought all the beggars back to the streets of our towns after sixty to seventy years. In this equally reasonable response, a specific appeal to undercurrents of passion is also being made. Those who attack beggars are themselves outrageously guilty. Guilt is being loaded back on to those attackers. Reversing the blame, by those who are outraged, is itself a method of getting out of the sense of responsibility and guilt by off-loading it into those unseemly attackers. However, piling guilt back on to those attackers meets people who have already found a means of loading their guilt elsewhere – on to the beggars. They will then be driven even further, and more persistently, to find the guilt in the beggars. Or, they may find another group to burden with guilt; soon after the aggressive beggar issue was started by the Prime Minister in 1994, Peter Lilley (the Social Services Minister) found a scandal with single mothers who had their babies simply to defraud the benefit system!

The issue of aggressive begging (and indeed single mothers) demonstrates important features. It has a reasonableness. Seemingly. However, it touches on a very different level. The level of passions. Those that concern painful guilt and responsibility in all of us. The deftness of the campaign was to render those feelings unfelt. Thus, an idea, presented as a purely social issue, was in fact also a heartfelt affair of the passions. The credence given to the idea that beggars are aggressive and unworthy is evaluated by the passions. Because it gives us relief.

The features to note are (a) the seemingly straightforward political presentations; (b) the intense emotional values that are stirred by the common painful feelings (guilt and responsibility); and (c) the inability, once carried away by the passions, to see that we are in fact being so carried away. In addition, it is worth noting that the reaction to the campaign against aggressive beggars is different according to which group one belongs to – supporting the campaign if you tend to be on the right politically, and outraged by it if you tend towards the left. Your social location matters.

Position

It seems such a good idea to preserve objectivity, neutrality and reason. If only it were possible. But, despite the lure we cannot, in fact, stand on the horizon of our own world and take a distanced view. We can only start from where we are. And the lure leads us to a certainty, but a mistaken certainty, about our position. It can only be a false objectivity, a fool's gold. That is false consciousness.

That position of standing aside and apart is unattainable, for classes, for nations, for gender, for races, for sects and so on. Whatever ideas we have and impart are always driven by the moment and the place. However enduring they prove eventually to be, they arise in a context and bear its traces.

How is history made?

We like to hope that we plan rationally for our future. We develop in an orderly way. Reason dominates. Yet is that so?

I claim that social prescription and planning (social engineering) subjugate people to the good idea. It is engineering of the following ilk: collectivise the peasants, or purify Germany by eradicating non-Aryan blood. In short it is ideological. And it is disastrous.

However, even those great projects of social planning of the 1930s, German National Socialism and Soviet Communism, have eventually succumbed to unplanned history. That is an important lesson.

History is not made that way.

The transformation of society which we are at present undergoing as a result of the silicon chip and its economic exploitation was not planned. History, the development of our society, is being made under our noses. We did not prescribe that some scientist somewhere be set going to invent virtual reality.

Instead it just happened. It is true that rational scientific thinking, rational judgements and planning went into it – but into the development of the technology. The impact on society is different, not predicted, unprescribed. We watch with fascination as the technology has changed us and the world we live in. We wonder how we will live, and our children will live, next century. This is history and it is not planned in itself. What *was* planned were the gadgets that could be built, played with and exploited economically.

To put our passion behind an idea that is supposed to stand outside of, or above, society is doomed in the long run – and great heartache is involved in the course of its rise and fall. The lesson of history is, in my view, the following: we cannot trust ourselves to be reasonable and objective, we can only rely on being blinkered and obstructed by passions we can barely acknowledge.

Incidentally, beware proclamations, even of this kind! You see, even that hypothesis – that we accept the uncontrolled waywardness of passions – can itself become an idea transported into an ideology. It could support the position of extreme libertarianism (the extreme right-wing anti-state dictatorship, an example of which has been pioneered so brilliantly for a decade and a half by recent Conservative governments). It proclaims the freedom to consume entirely according to one's whims and passions. And yet that idea gives rise to woeful restrictions of freedom, arising from poverty, homelessness and exploitative social relations. The ideology of libertarianism has spawned such oppression that a doomed fate for this idea is sealed. The victorious ideology of the market, which ran its course in the eighteenth and nineteenth centuries, now appears to be doing so all over again.

Searching for solutions

The problem is: what else can we do?

There are currently two competing methods for overcoming this headlong rush into a group obsession. One is to acknowledge that there is no objectivity; we are all of us in our own small worlds. This is pluralism, and it neglects the fact that pulsing undercurrents of passion intrude into reason. The other is a lofty neutrality that disdains passions, but claims a global consciousness. In fact, both are partial solutions and therefore each in its own way is fallible.

Pluralism: First, is the campaign to allow us our differences? We must legislate for that. Throughout the twentieth century one political strand of opinion has asserted democratic, egalitarian or pluralistic alternatives. They erect, self-consciously, the welfare of human beings, not ideas, as the objective of politics. Everyone should have his or her say in our multicultured, multilayered societies of the West. Minority pressure groups, single-issue politics, liberation movements create a rich mosaic of political life. But it is one which has become increasingly difficult to develop consensus in. Each small tessera is, as it were, freed from its glue. The mosaic becomes a glittering but unstable kaleidoscope. It is one in which there is a constant rubbing up against the sharp edges of someone else's obsession. Currently, we are fatefully depressed by the dominance of *this* ideology, political correctness: I cannot, as a man, have a word about women and their place in society without being disenfranchised just because I am a man – unless my words are in the form and content of women's rhetoric; I have to become as it were an honorary woman, but only by permission.

The advantages of being in one of such a 'minority' group is that it gives a full entitlement to its members to have ideas about everyone else, while mounting an intimidation against the entitlement of anyone else to have a say. Pluralism, from praiseworthy motives, can degenerate into a remarkably familiar factionalism.

Neutrality: In contrast, this is a more conservative, or patrician, stance. If there is a squabble, then the best position is to be on the fence, umpiring it. This is admirable. It has a note of conviction about it, the sensible person – sane and rational weighing up the pros and cons: the far right or the centre right, the state versus privatisation, the European currency or a federation of nation states... Dispassionate judgement of this kind sounds the right sort of thing to bring temperance to political debate; and if only there were enough people who could create a central balance in this way we could be rescued from extremism, from the suppurating rancour between factions...and so on.

This kind of argument against vehement political debate is common. It receives a considerable impetus from other activities in life where such neutral objectivity appears really to deliver the goods: in scientific research for instance; in the law courts; even in the proclamations of rational management in industry; and possibly in the non-judgemental attitude of the psychotherapist faced with his patient's internal conflicts of passion. In English culture of the last hundred years (at least in middle-class culture), the stiffness of the upper lip is a hallmark of resistance to the encroachments of passion upon reason. We are brought up to the resounding good sense of a neutral objectivity.

Given all this, why, then, is political debate so very far removed from this ideal? The cacophony in the House of Commons which we can now see on our televisions never reaches the sophistication of even student debates in university. There is an answer to this question. And the answer is that objective neutrality cannot be achieved, not by human beings at any rate. The nearest approximation to it is to disown one's own impassioned impulses and evaluations and see them only as the frail weaknesses of others, there to condemn them. Given the evidence of passions in political life, passionless neutrality seems a sensible goal. But neutrality is a kind of personal violence to oneself, a severing of that energy that makes us human rather than machine-like. And the result is unexpected. Reasons and passions get intermingled in ways that are uncontrolled and unconscious. Reason gets confused by unacknowledged passions; and we distract our attention from these values given by our passions through trying to (and believing we can) adopt a position of objectivity and neutrality.

Creative solutions

It is time to address the possibility of more constructive solutions. We may not be condemned to meander within this dichotomy swayed helplessly by passions, or stiffly superior with a wooden, neutral reasonableness. Despite reservations about these contrasting mistakes, we can do nothing about the fact that human beings are passionate – however rational they might also be. One distinctive contribution that psychoanalysis has made is to understand that passion and passionate assertions of ideas are everywhere, all of the time. Not just rational assertions of them.

Therefore, any exhortation to reasonableness cannot succeed unless we are familiar with, and have a vocabulary for, the throbbing of the human heart. Psychoanalysis has the materials to begin to understand those processes. But the field of operations of psychoanalysis is the heart of the individual not that of the collective. We need then to be careful about transferring our knowledge from the therapeutic setting to the social one. And the big difference is that the psychoanalyst provides himself with a carefully arranged situation in which he has some chance of keeping a part of his mind in a state in which he can reflect (as best he can) on what happens between him and his patient. Outside that very special setting, and in the spinning confusion of ordinary social processes, the psychoanalyst and psychotherapist are as lost among those currents as anyone else.

The question is: can we change our collective operation of belief systems and values so that groups, factions, classes can live together in a different way? Can we overcome the blinkered reactions to unacknowledged emotions, values, desires that are specific to location?

Recent history – this century of planning by ideas – emphasises that no planning can avoid being ideological. But what other urge to the future can there be which is not planning by ideas? To demonstrate one instance would be to open up a chink of a possibility for finding a route around ideology, the possibility of a different kind of politics. It is enough, here, to demonstrate it is possible. We will have to leave for further work a fuller picture of what a politics of such a grouping might become.

If, currently, political groupings are welded together by the 'good idea' – about the market, about a planned economy, about fair-minded pluralism, about fundamentalism of various kinds – are there other kinds of groupings, somewhere, that are held together by something else? What sorts of collective are there which are not held by an 'idea'? And are they as malignant?

We seek something that is not necessarily rational, nor even necessarily conscious. This might be some 'thing' of the kind to which psychoanalysts could contribute, because they are more at home with the unconscious and less likely to be suspicious or scared of it.

The creative impulse. Let us consider the creative impulse. Wordsworth and Coleridge produced their *Lyrical Ballads* in 1790, as a joint enterprise. They, together with Wordsworth's sister Dorothy, formed a group that expressed very consciously their revolt against prescribed rules, and held to a belief in the pre-eminence of emotions, especially those subtle emotions evoked in the play of nature upon the senses.

Another collective identity was achieved in the early work of the Cubist painters. The works of Picasso and Braque of this period are almost impossible to distinguish from each other. They formed an identification with each other so great that their work was identical.

Neither the early Romantics nor the Cubists were devoid of ideas. But as collectives, they were not drawn together by their rational ideas. Instead they came together in ways which balanced their ideas with other aspects. In particular it was the urge to create. Those collectives each changed the future of Western culture – not as a planned idea, but as a creative urge.

Possibly the most creative of all activities engaged in between human beings is the creation of a new human life, a baby. Sex, for all its exploitability, is an impulse for the future. The family therefore represents, too, a kind of grouping based on a creative impulse.

I do not intend to go very far along this path. It is, in any case, something to be done collectively. Perhaps, too, it is not very new. And indeed it might be more like an ancient footpath which has become difficult to follow because it is now so overgrown. And it is overgrown because the more inviting and well-travelled path in our culture is the rational, instrumental (especially for economic ends) and objective approach.

But I claim that these little glimmers of possibility indicate that we, human beings, can come together in collectives that are not based on ideology. It is enough to claim a new kind of political future is possible. It could, I claim, be worth exploring.

Perhaps even these movements can become 'good ideas', ones which are economically exploited. The creative urge could itself become an 'idea' and a pressing ideology as some later Romantics, especially Byron, proved. It is, then, an over-emphasis on the pre-eminence of the sensual emotional life over reason that overbalanced the Romantic movement, the idea of passionate life. If so, it is once again a pointer to the failings that erupt from moving too far to one side or the other on the see-saw of emotions versus reason.

Initially, the creative push forward, the ones I have mentioned, relied on intuition, not reason. They were descriptive, not prescriptive. They described a state of mind or mood, they did not prescribe an ideal condition to be. Is this too the quality of a psychoanalyst's interpretation? – intuitive descriptions of a patient's narrative, rather than prescriptive instructions of his cure.

To be sure these groupings – whether cultural production or physical reproduction – can be thought about. We can have ideas about them.

Reasons and values

Let us contrast this with the process I began with. An idea is given emotional value through identifications within a social group. It is transformed by that social process into an ideology held with a consuming passion. And the passionate evaluation of rational ideas proceeds, unthinkingly, to political levels.

Now, instead of passions giving value to ideas, I think we might begin to see a possibility of rational evaluation of passions (passions which take the form, for instance, of creativity). This is to assume a different level. Clearly there is a danger that this gets into the same difficulties as the arching assumption of reasoned generalities from outside that I described earlier. However, if it is true that passions are of a moment and of a place, then rational evaluation of them could be more grounded. Such a stooping posture would therefore need to be continually worked for: reason tied to a moment.

Moreover, a level that will encompass and frame those collective evaluations is not merely a psychology, which stands outside and looks in on people, but rather it comprises a level for addressing the collective – a political level. This means a search for a political expression of the passionate and intuitive side of human collectives.

To be sure, political thinking must comprise the rational debate on our material and objective needs – and how they may be justly and equably supplied. But it need not be a political discourse that arouses or exploits emotional evaluations; instead we can envisage a political accounting of our emotional life and needs as well as material ones. Therefore political discourse demands a literacy of the emotions and intuitions, one which complements the discourse on our bodily needs.

Of what might a political literacy of the emotions consist?

Needs and justice. 'Man,' the Bible says, 'cannot live by bread alone.' The rational provision of material bodily needs has to be augmented by the emotional provision for a person's psychological needs – in particular the need for a profound identification with a group.

Collectively we need to supply each other with more than our material needs. We have emotional needs of each other, and these needs are not merely for pleasure, but equally (perhaps more so) for the sense of being a person, and what sort of person. All our emotional needs are aroused and soothed by being a part of each other in our groups and societies. The political life of our society should attend to those psychological needs as well as to the economic supply of material ones.

Unlike material provision for each other, our emotional needs cannot be supplied under the principle of distributive justice nor, obviously, by any kind of market. Our need to identify with a group can – should – become a political end, and not just a means of politicking.

We need our new framework to supplement collectively our emotional needs in a way that has hardly been considered in the past. When George Orwell (*Down and Out in Paris and London*) and William Henry Davies (*Autobiography of a Super-Tramp*), in the 1930s, actually joined the beggars on their travels they were involved in a political act of solidarity for the plight of tramps. It was more than just a distanced plea for better material provision and welfare. They accomplished an emotional step of going right into the lives of beggars. They identified, and survived. That solidarity of becoming is a different kind of political act. Yet it is in a sense a rather crude one. Can we not identify in ways that are reflective as well as active, while remaining genuine enough? We do not have to become a beggar in order to discover the emotional interplay within the issue of aggressive begging. Or, do we? I claim we can know – through an act of intuitive reflection, 'knowing what it feels like'. That is a political act too.

Locking into another's needs without becoming invasive, and while remaining also oneself, is an art that the psychoanalyst practises. It is a truly collective politics. The emotional needs of the human being are mediated always through others. Such needs are in fact more truly collective (and therefore political) than are the individual needs of the material body. Having, now, as a society, the wherewithal largely to supply our physical needs, we must embark on a search for a politics that can address the emotional cravings and sufferings which we so blithely relegate to personal obscurity. For the neglect of our emotional needs is at the root of the failure to provide justly for material needs.

Conclusions

It is a sweeping statement to say that all social planning puts ideas above people. And yet that is the hypothesis this essay has set out to investigate. We have to brace ourselves for a severe cultural U-turn, to seek a politics of awareness, and of description – and let fall our politics of prescription and ideological objectivity. This essay has not been, whatever else, a polemical tract on behalf of a new idea.

I have wanted to experiment with a different level – one about *the way of conducting* political debate and how argument could take place. If we shift from being people with ideas, to become people who are mindful of the way we have our ideas, then we must shift from our Western view-from-the-outside stance on people. In effect, we must all be psychologists. And this book is about the way one strand of psychology, psychoanalysis and psychotherapy, can inform us about taking that new position.

As psychoanalysts and psychotherapists we do know something about our needs for emotional identifications (and distances). Group therapists and analysts know of the collective power of ideas, which are driven by hidden passions. And we have seen how political debate as it is currently conducted mingles reasons and hidden emotional values in a specific way.

A new politics has to start by unravelling that tangled knot. We must proceed by giving equal place to emotional needs and material ones. We must, finally, achieve a thoughtful container for our emotional imperatives while avoiding the relapse into a passionate espousal of proud ideas.

References

Armstrong, D. (1991) *The Institution in the Mind: Reflections on the Relations of Psychoanalysis to Work with Institutions*. London: Grubb Institute.

Asch, S. (1952) *Social Psychology*. Englewood Cliffs, NJ: Prentice-Hall.

Barnes, T. (2000) 'The legacy of therapeutic community practice in modern community mental health services.' *Therapeutic Communities 21*, 165–174.

Barnes, E., Griffiths, P., Old, J. and Wells, D. (1997) *Face-to-Face with Distress*. London: Butterworth-Heinemann.

Baron, C. (1987) *From Asylum to Anarchy*. London: Free Association Books.

Barratt, R. (1996) *The Psychiatric Team and the Social Definition of Schizophrenia*. Cambridge: Cambridge University Press.

Bauman, Z. (1995) *Life in Fragments*. Oxford: Blackwell.

Berlin, I. (1958) 'Two concepts of liberty.' In *Four Essays of Liberty*. Oxford: Oxford University Press.

Bierer, J. and Evans, R. (1969) *Innovations in Social Psychiatry*. London: Avenue Publishing.

Bion, W. R. (1957) 'Differentiation of the psychotic from the non-psychotic part of the personality.' *International Journal of Psycho-Analysis 38*, 266–275. Reprinted in W. R. Bion (1967) *Second Thoughts*. London: Heinemann. And republished 1988 in Elizabeth Bott Spillius (ed) *Melanie Klein Today, Volume 1*. London: Routledge.

Bion, W. R. (1959) 'Attacks on linking.' *International Journal of Psycho-Analysis 40*, 308–315. Reprinted in W. R. Bion (1967) *Second Thoughts*. London: Heinemann. And republished 1988 in Elizabeth Bott Spillius (ed) *Melanie Klein Today, Volume 1*. London: Routledge.

Bion, W. R. (1961) *Experiences in Groups*. London: Tavistock.

Bion, W. R. (1962) *Learning from Experience*. London: Heinemann.

Bion, W. R. (1970) *Attention and Interpretation*. London: Tavistock.

Bion, W. R. and Rickman, J. (1943) 'Intra-group tensions in therapy.' *Lancet 1943 ii*, 678–681. Reprinted in W. R. Bion (1961) *Experiences in Groups*. London: Tavistock.

Bott Spillius, E. (1976) 'Hospital and society.' *British Journal of Medical Psychology* *49*, 97–140. Revised 1990 as 'Asylum and society.' In E. Trist and H. Murray (eds) *The Social Engagement of Social Science, Volume 1*. London: Free Association Books.

Britton, R. (1989) 'The missing link.' In R. Britton, M. Feldman and E. O'Shaughnessy, *The Oedipus Complex Today*. London: Karnac.

Busfield, J. (1986) *Managing Madness: Changing Ideas and Practice*. London: Hutchinson.

Christian, A. and Hinshelwood, R. D. (1979) 'Work Groups.' In R. D. Hinshelwood and N. Manning (eds) *Therapeutic Communities: Reflections and Progress*. London: Routledge.

Clark, D. (1964) *Administrative Therapy*. London: Tavistock.

Clark, D. (1965) 'Therapeutic community, concept, practice and future.' *British Journal of Psychiatry 111*, 947–954.

Clark, D. (1996) *The Story of a Mental Hospital*. London: Process Press.

Cooper, D. (1967) *Psychiatry and Anti-Psychiatry*. London: Tavistock.

Day, L. and Pringle, P. (2001) *Cassel Monograph. No2*. London: Karnac.

Donati, F. (1989) 'A psychodynamic observer in a chronic psychiatric ward.' *British Journal of Psychotherapy 5*, 317–329. Republished in R. D. Hinshelwood and W. Skogstad (eds) (2000) *Observing Organisations*. London: Routledge.

Featherstone, M. (1990) *Consumer Culture and Postmodernism*. London: Sage.

Foster, A. (1998a) 'Thinking about risk.' In A. Foster and V. Z. Roberts (eds) *Managing Mental Health in the Community: Chaos and Containment*. London: Routledge.

Foster, A. (1998b) 'Psychotic processes and community care.' In A. Foster and V. Z. Roberts (eds) *Managing Mental Health in the Community: Chaos and Containment*. London: Routledge.

Foster, A. and Roberts, V. Z. (eds) (1998) *Managing Mental Health in the Community: Chaos and Containment*. London: Routledge.

Foulkes, S. H. (1975) *Group Analytic Psychotherapy: Method and Principles*. London: Gordon and Bridge.

Foulkes, S. H. and Anthony, J. (1957) *Group Psychotherapy*. London: Penguin.

Freud, S. (1909) 'Analysis of a phobia in a five-year-old boy.' *The Standard Edition of the Complete Psychological Works of Sigmund Freud 10*. London: Hogarth.

Freud, S. (1913) *Totem and Taboo. The Standard Edition of the Complete Psychological Works of Sigmund Freud 13*. London: Hogarth.

Freud, S. (1930) *Civilisation and its Discontents. The Standard Edition of the Complete Psychological Works of Sigmund Freud 21*. London: Hogarth.

Fulford, W. (1989) *Moral Theory and Medical Practice.* Cambridge: Cambridge University Press.

Gillon, R. (1986) *Philosophical Medical Ethics.* Chichester: John Wiley.

Goffman, I. (1968) *Asylums.* London: Penguin.

Gomez, L. (1997) *An Introduction to Object Relations.* London: Free Association Books.

Griffiths, P. and Hinshelwood, R. D. (1997) 'Actions speak louder than words.' In P. Griffiths and P. Pringle (1997) *Cassel Monograph No.1 – Psychosocial Practice within a Residential Setting.* London: Karnac.

Griffiths, P. and Hinshelwood, R. D. (2001) 'A culture of enquiries: life in a hall of mirrors.' In L. Day and P. Pringle, *Cassel Monograph No.2.* London: Karnac.

Griffiths, P. and Pringle, P. (1997) *Cassel Monograph No.1 – Psychosocial Practice within a Residential Setting.* London: Karnac.

Grunberg, S. (1979) 'Thinking and the development of structure in a community group.' In R. D. Hinshelwood and Nick Manning (eds) *Therapeutic Communities: Reflections and Progress.* London: Routledge.

Harrison, T. (2000) *Rickman, Bion, Foulkes and the Northfield Experiments.* London: Jessica Kingsley Publishers.

Haynal, A. (1988) *The Technique at Issue.* London: Karnac.

Heimann, P. (1950) 'On counter-transference.' *International Journal of Psycho-Analysis 31,* 81–84.

Heimann, P. (1952) 'Certain functions of introjection and projection in early infancy.' In M. Klein, P. Heimann, S. Issacs and J. Riviere, *Developments in Psycho-Analysis.* London: Hogarth.

Hinshelwood, R. D. (1979a) 'The community as analyst.' In R. D. Hinshelwood and N. Manning (eds) *Therapeutic Communities: Reflections and Progress.* London: Routledge.

Hinshelwood, R. D. (1979b) 'Supervision as an exchange system.' In R. D. Hinshelwood and N. Manning (eds) *Therapeutic Communities: Reflections and Progress.* London: Routledge.

Hinshelwood, R. D. (1979c) 'Demoralisation in the hospital community.' *Group-Analysis 12,* 84–93.

Hinshelwood, R. D. (1982) 'The individual and the social network.' In M. Pines and L. Raphaelson (eds) *The Individual and the Group, Volume 1.* London: Plenum, pp.469–477.

Hinshelwood, R. D. (1983) 'Projective identification and Marx's concept of man.' *International Review of Psycho-Analysis 10,* 221–226.

Hinshelwood, R. D. (1987a) *What Happens in Groups.* London: Free Association Books.

Hinshelwood, R. D. (1987b) 'Social dynamics and individual symptoms.' *International Journal of Therapeutic Communities 8,* 265–272.

Hinshelwood, R. D. (1989a) *A Dictionary of Kleinian Thought.* London: Free Association Books.

Hinshelwood, R. D. (1989b) 'The therapeutic community in a changing social and cultural environment.' *International Journal of Therapeutic Communities 10,* 63–69.

Hinshelwood, R. D. (1989c) 'The social possession of identity.' In B. Richards (ed) *Crisis of the Self.* London: Free Association Books.

Hinshelwood, R. D. (1989d) 'Communication flow in the matrix.' *Group Analysis 22,* 261–269.

Hinshelwood, R. D. (1993a) 'Locked in role.' *Journal of Forensic Psychiatry 4,* 427–440.

Hinshelwood, R. D. (1993b) *Clinical Klein.* London: Free Association Books.

Hinshelwood, R. D. (1994a) 'Integrity of the person and the day hospital: evidence from a therapeutic community.' *International Journal of Therapeutic Communities 15,* 29–38.

Hinshelwood, R. D. (1994b) 'Attacks on the reflective space.' In V. Shermer and M. Pines (eds) *Ring of Fire.* London: Routledge.

Hinshelwood, R. D. (1995) 'The social relocation of personal identity.' *Philosophy, Psychology, Psychiatry 2,* 185–204.

Hinshelwood, R. D. (1996a) 'Convergences with psycho-analysis.' In I. Parker and R. Spiers (eds) *Psychology and Marxism.* London: Pluto Press.

Hinshelwood, R. D. (1996b) 'Communities and their health.' *Therapeutic Communities 17,* 173–182.

Hinshelwood, R.D. (1996c) 'I have an idea…' In D. Kennard and N. Small (eds) *Living Together.* London: Quartet.

Hinshelwood, R. D. (1997a) *Therapy or Coercion: Does Psychoanalysis Differ from Brainwashing?* London: Karnac.

Hinshelwood, R. D. (1997b) 'Primitive mental processes: psycho-analysis and the ethics of integration.' *Philosophy, Psychology, Psychiatry 4,* 121–143.

Hinshelwood, R. D. (1998) 'Creatures of each other: some historical considerations of responsibility and care and some present undercurrents.' In A. Foster and V. Z. Roberts (eds) *Managing Mental Health in the Community: Chaos and Containment in Community Care.* London: Routledge.

Hinshelwood, R. D. (1999a) 'The Difficult Patient.' *British Journal of Psychiatry 174,* 187–190.

Hinshelwood, R. D. (1999b) 'How Foulkesian was Bion?' *Group-Analysis 32,* 469–488.

Hinshelwood, R. D. (2000) 'Alienation: social relations and therapeutic relations.' *Psychoanalytic Studies 2*, 21–30.

Hinshelwood, R. D. (2001) 'Group mentality and having a mind.' In M. Pines and R. Lipgar (eds) *Beyond Bion* (in preparation).

Hinshelwood, R. D. and Grunberg, S. (1979) 'The large group syndrome.' In R. D. Hinshelwood and N. Manning (eds) *Therapeutic Communities: Reflections and Progress*. London: Routledge and Kegan Paul.

Hinshelwood, R. D. and Skogstad, W. (1998) 'The hospital in the mind: in-patient psychotherapy at the Cassel Hospital.' In J. Pestalozzi, S. Frisch, R. D. Hinshelwood and D. Houzel (eds) *Psychoanalytic Psychotherapy in Institutional Settings*. London: Karnac.

Hinshelwood, R. D. and Skogstad, W. (eds) (2000) *Observing Organisations*. London: Routledge.

Hirschhorn, L. (1995) *The Workplace Within: Psychodynamics of Organizational Life*. Cambridge, MA: MIT Press.

Holden, H. (1972) 'On doing the washing-up.' Marlborough Day Hospital, privately circulated paper.

Inskip, H. (1976) Report. South East Thames Regional Health Authority.

Jackson, M. and Williams, P. (1994) *Unimaginable Storms*. London: Karnac.

James, O. (1987) 'The role of the nurse/therapist relationship in a therapeutic community.' In R. Kennedy, A. Heymans and L. Tischler (eds) *The Family as In-Patient*. London: Free Association Books.

Jaques, E. (1951) *The Changing Culture of a Factory*. London: Tavistock.

Jaques, E. (1953) 'On the dynamics of social structure.' *Human Relations 6*, 10–23. Republished in revised form, 1955, as 'The social system as a defence against persecutory and depressive anxiety.' In M. Klein, P. Heimann and R. Money-Kyrle (eds) *New Directions in Psycho-Analysis*. London: Tavistock.

Jones, M.(1952) *Social Psychiatry: A Study of Therapeutic Communities*. London: Tavistock.

Jones, M., Pomryn, B. A. and Skellern, E. (1956) 'Work therapy.' *Lancet 1*, 343–344.

Jones, M. (1968) *Social Psychiatry in Practice*. London: Penguin.

Kemshall, H. and Pritchard, J. (eds) (1996) *Good Practice in Risk Assessment and Risk Management*. London: Jessica Kingsley Publishers.

Kennard, D. (1999) Preface to the First Edition (1983) *Introduction to Therapeutic Communities*. London: Jessica Kingsley Publishers.

Kennard, D. and Small, N. (1996) *Living Together*. London: Quartet.

Kennedy, R. (1987) 'The work of the day.' In R. Kennedy, A. Heymans and L. Tischler (eds) *The Family as In-Patient*. London: Free Association Books.

Republished in P. Griffiths and P. Pringle (1998) *Psychosocial Practice within a Residential Setting.* London: Karnac.

Kennedy, R. (1993) *Freedom to Relate.* London: Free Association Books.

Klein, M. (1932) *The Psycho-Analysis of Children.* Republished as *The Writings of Melanie Klein, Volume 2.* London: Hogarth.

Klein, M. (1946) 'Notes on some schizoid mechanisms.' In *The Writings of Melanie Klein, Volume 3.* London: Hogarth.

Laing, R. D. (1959) *The Divided Self.* London: Tavistock.

van den Langenberg, S. and de Nastris, P. (1985) 'A narrow escape from the Magic Mountain.' *International Journal of Therapeutic Communities 6*, 91–101.

LeBon, G. (1895) *Psychologie des Foulkes.* Paris: Alean.

Leff, J. (1997) *Care in the Community: Illusion or Reality.* Chichester: John Wiley.

Main, T. F. (1946) 'The Hospital as a Therapeutic Institution.' *Bulletin of the Menninger Clinic 10*, 66–70. Republished in T. F. Main (1989) *The Ailment and Other Psychoanalytic Essays.* London: Free Association Books.

Main, T. F. (1967) 'Knowledge, learning and freedom from thought.' *The Australian and New Zealand Journal of Psychiatry 1*, 64–71. Reprinted 1990 in *Psychoanalytic Psychotherapy 15*, 59–74.

Main, T. F. (1975) 'Some psychodynamics of large groups.' In Lionel Kreeger (ed) *The Large Group.* London: Constable.

Main, T. F. (1977) 'The concept of the therapeutic community: variations and vicissitudes.' *Group-Analysis 10*, 2–17. Reprinted 1983 in M. Pines (ed) *The Evolution of Group Analysis.* London: Routledge and Kegan Paul. Republished in T. F. Main (1995) *The Ailment and Other Psychoanalytic Essays.* London: Free Association Books.

Mandelbrote, B. (1965) 'The use of psychodynamic and sociodynamic principles in the treatment of psychotics.' *Comprehensive Psychiatry 6*, 381–387.

Manning, N. (1989) *The Therapeutic Community Movement: Charisma and Routinization.* London: Routledge.

Martin, D. (1955) 'Institutionalisation.' *Lancet 1955 ii*, 1188–1190.

Marx, K. (1844) *Economic and philosopical manuscripts.* In *Early Writings, 1975*, London: Penguin.

Menzies, I. E. P. (1959) 'A case study in the functioning of social systems as a defence against anxiety.' *Human Relations 13*, 95–121. Reprinted in E. Trist and H. Murray (eds) (1990) *The Social Engagement of Social Science, Volume 1.* London: Free Association Books.

Menzies, I. E. P. (1979) 'Staff Support Systems.' In R. D. Hinshelwood and N. Manning (eds) *Therapeutic Communities: Reflections and Progress.* London: Routledge and Kegan Paul.

Menzies, I. E. P. (1988a) 'A psychoanalytic perspective on social institutions.' In E. Bott Spillius (ed) *Melanie Klein Today, Volume 2: Mainly Practice.* London: Free Association Books.

Menzies, I. E. P. (1988b) 'The interaction between Epsom and the five mental hospitals adjoining it.' Verbal report on the findings given at a meeting held at the South West Metropolitan Regional Hospital Board, 10th September 1968. Published in I. E. P. Menzies (1989) *The Dynamics of the Social.* London: Free Association Books.

Meyer, D. (1969) 'Resistances to occupational therapy.' *British Journal of Occupational Therapy 32,* 39–42.

Milgram, S. (1969) *Obedience to Authority.* New York: Harper and Row.

Milner, M. (J. Field) (1950) *On Not Being Able to Paint.* London: Heinemann.

Morris, M. (2000) 'Tyrannical equality: a mental health hostel.' In R. D. Hinshelwood and W. Skogstad (eds) (2000) *Observing Organisations.* London: Routledge.

Nathan, J. (1998) 'The psychic organisation of community care.' In Angela Foster and V. Z. Roberts (eds) *Managing Mental Health in the Community: Chaos and Containment.* London: Routledge.

Norton, K. (1992) 'A culture of enquiry – its preservation or loss.' *Therapeutic Communities 13,* 3–25.

Norton, K. and Hinshelwood, R. D. (1996) 'Severe personality disorder: treatment issues and selection for in-patient psychotherapy.' *British Journal of Psychiatry 168,* 723–731.

Obholzer, A. and Roberts, V. Z. (1994) *The Unconscious at Work.* London: Routledge.

Punch, M. (1974) 'The sociology of the anti-institution.' *British Journal of Sociology 25,* 312–325.

Rapaport, R. (1960) *Community as Doctor.* London: Tavistock.

Roberts, J. (1982) 'Foulkes's concept of the matrix.' *Group-Analysis 15,* 111–126.

Rosenberg, S. D. (1970) 'Hospital culture as a collective defence.' *Psychiatry 33,* 21–38.

Santos, A. and Hinshelwood, R. D. (1998) 'The use at the Cassel of the organisational dynamics to enhance the therapeutic work.' *Therapeutic Communities 19,* 29–39.

Schoenberg, E. (ed) (1972) *A Hospital Looks at Itself.* London: Cassirer.

Segal, H. (1957) 'Notes on symbol formation.' *International Journal of Psycho-Analysis 38,* 391–397. Republished in H. Segal (1981) *The Works of Hanna Segal.* New York: J. Aronson. And in E. Bott Spillius (ed) (1988) *Melanie Klein Today, Volume 1.* London: Routledge.

Segal, H. (1975) 'A psychoanalytic approach to the treatment of schizophrenia.' In M. Lader (ed) *Studies in Schizophrenia*. Ashford: Headley Brothers. Republished in H. Segal (1981) *The Works of Hanna Segal*. New York: Jason Aronson.

Segal, H. (1977) *Psycho-Analysis and Freedom of Thought*. London: H. K. Lewis. Republished in H. Segal (1981) *The Works of Hanna Segal*. New York: Jason Aronson.

Shenker, B. (1986) *Intentional Communities*. London: Routledge.

Stanton, A. and Schwartz, M. (1954) *The Mental Hospital*. New York: Basic Books.

Stapley, L. (1996) *The Personality of the Organisation*. London: Free Association Books.

Stokes, J. (1994) 'The unconscious at work in groups and teams.' In A. Obholzer and V. Z. Roberts (eds) *The Unconscious at Work*. London: Routledge.

Strathern, M. (2000) *Audit Cultures*. London: Routledge.

Szasz, T. (1961) *The Myth of Mental Illness*. New York: Hoeber-Harper.

Taylor, C. (1989) *The Sources of the Self*. Cambridge: Cambridge University Press.

Turner, V. (1969) *The Ritual Process*. London: Routledge and Kegan Paul.

Turquet, P. (1975) 'Threats to identity in the large group.' In L. Kreeger (ed) *The Large Group*. London: Constable.

Young, R. (1985) *Darwin's Metaphor*. Cambridge: Cambridge University Press.

Subject Index

209

Author Index